T0301969

An Analysis of

Michael E. Porter's

Competitive Strategy
Techniques for Analyzing
Industries and Competitors

Pádraig Belton

Published by Macat International Ltd
24:13 Coda Centre, 189 Munster Road, London SW6 6AW.

Distributed exclusively by Routledge
2 Park Square, Milton Park, Abingdon, Oxon OX14 4RN
711 Third Avenue, New York, NY 10017, USA

Routledge is an imprint of the Taylor & Francis Group, an informa business

www.macat.com
info@macat.com

Cataloguing in Publication Data
A catalogue record for this book is available from the British Library.
Library of Congress Cataloguing-in-Publication Data is available upon request.
Cover illustration: Etienne Gilfillan

ISBN 978-1-912302-18-5 (hardback)
ISBN 978-1-912128-80-8 (paperback)
ISBN 978-1-912281-06-0 (e-book)

Notice
The information in this book is designed to orientate readers of the work under analysis,
to elucidate and contextualise its key ideas and themes, and to aid in the development
of critical thinking skills. It is not meant to be used, nor should it be used, as a
substitute for original thinking or in place of original writing or research. References and
notes are provided for informational purposes and their presence does not constitute
endorsement of the information or opinions therein. This book is presented solely for
educational purposes. It is sold on the understanding that the publisher is not engaged
to provide any scholarly advice. The publisher has made every effort to ensure that
this book is accurate and up-to-date, but makes no warranties or representations with
regard to the completeness or reliability of the information it contains. The information
and the opinions provided herein are not guaranteed or warranted to produce particular
results and may not be suitable for students of every ability. The publisher shall not be
liable for any loss, damage or disruption arising from any errors or omissions, or from
the use of this book, including, but not limited to, special, incidental, consequential or
other damages caused, or alleged to have been caused, directly or indirectly, by the
information contained within.

CONTENTS

THE MACAT LIBRARY

The Macat Library is a series of unique academic explorations of seminal works in the humanities and social sciences – books and papers that have had a significant and widely recognised impact on their disciplines. It has been created to serve as much more than just a summary of what lies between the covers of a great book. It illuminates and explores the influences on, ideas of, and impact of that book. Our goal is to offer a learning resource that encourages critical thinking and fosters a better, deeper understanding of important ideas.

Each publication is divided into three Sections: Influences, Ideas, and Impact. Each Section has four Modules. These explore every important facet of the work, and the responses to it.

This Section-Module structure makes a Macat Library book easy to use, but it has another important feature. Because each Macat book is written to the same format, it is possible (and encouraged!) to cross-reference multiple Macat books along the same lines of inquiry or research. This allows the reader to open up interesting interdisciplinary pathways.

To further aid your reading, lists of glossary terms and people mentioned are included at the end of this book (these are indicated by an asterisk [*] throughout) – as well as a list of works cited.

Macat has worked with the University of Cambridge to identify the elements of critical thinking and understand the ways in which six different skills combine to enable effective thinking.
Three allow us to fully understand a problem; three more give us the tools to solve it. Together, these six skills make up the **PACIER** model of critical thinking. They are:

ANALYSIS – understanding how an argument is built
EVALUATION – exploring the strengths and weaknesses of an argument
INTERPRETATION – understanding issues of meaning

CREATIVE THINKING – coming up with new ideas and fresh connections
PROBLEM-SOLVING – producing strong solutions
REASONING – creating strong arguments

To find out more, visit **WWW.MACAT.COM.**

CRITICAL THINKING AND *COMPETITIVE STRATEGY*

Primary critical thinking skill: EVALUATION
Secondary critical thinking skill: ANALYSIS

Michael E. Porter's 1980 book *Competitive Strategy* is a fine example of critical thinking skills in action. Porter used his strong evaluative skills to overturn much of the accepted wisdom in the world of business. By exploring the strengths and weaknesses of the accepted argument that the best policy for firms to become more successful was to focus on expanding their market share, he was able to establish that the credibility of the argument was flawed. Porter did not believe such growth was the only way for a company to be successful, and provided compelling arguments as to why this was not the case. His book shows how industries can be fragmented, with different firms serving different parts of the market (the low-price mass market, and the expensive high-end market in clothing, for example) and examines strategies that businesses can follow in emerging, mature, and declining markets. If printing is in decline, for example, there may still be a market in this industry for high-end goods and services such as luxury craft bookbinding.

Porter also made excellent use of the critical thinking skill of analysis in writing *Competitive Strategy*. His advice that executives should analyze the five forces that mold the environment in which they compete – new entrants, substitute products, buyers, suppliers, and industry rivals – focused heavily on defining the relationships between these disparate factors and urged readers to check the assumptions of their arguments. Porter avoided technical jargon and wrote in a straightforward way to help readers see that his evaluation of the problem was strong. *Competitive Strategy* went on to be a highly influential work in the world of business strategy.

ABOUT THE AUTHOR OF THE ORIGINAL WORK

Michael E. Porter was born in 1947 into an American army family and lived in a number of different parts of the world while growing up. In secondary school and university he excelled in competitive sports, especially baseball, football, and golf. Porter earned an undergraduate degree in aerospace and mechanical engineering at Princeton University in 1969, graduating first in his class, and then went on to Harvard University for an MBA and a PhD in business economics. He then started lecturing at the Harvard Business School. Since 2001, Porter has directed Harvard's Institute for Strategy and Competitiveness. He is also one of the best-known academics in business and economics.

ABOUT THE AUTHOR OF THE ANALYSIS

Pádraig Belton undertook his doctoral research in politics and international relations at the University of Oxford. A prolific financial, business and political journalist, his work has appeared in publications including the *Irish Times, the Guardian, Telegraph, Independent, the Irish Independent, The Atlantic, the New Statesman, Prospect, The Times Literary Supplement,* and *Foreign Policy.*

ABOUT MACAT

GREAT WORKS FOR CRITICAL THINKING

Macat is focused on making the ideas of the world's great thinkers accessible and comprehensible to everybody, everywhere, in ways that promote the development of enhanced critical thinking skills.

It works with leading academics from the world's top universities to produce new analyses that focus on the ideas and the impact of the most influential works ever written across a wide variety of academic disciplines. Each of the works that sit at the heart of its growing library is an enduring example of great thinking. But by setting them in context – and looking at the influences that shaped their authors, as well as the responses they provoked – Macat encourages readers to look at these classics and game-changers with fresh eyes. Readers learn to think, engage and challenge their ideas, rather than simply accepting them.

'Macat offers an amazing first-of-its-kind tool for interdisciplinary learning and research. Its focus on works that transformed their disciplines and its rigorous approach, drawing on the world's leading experts and educational institutions, opens up a world-class education to anyone.'

Andreas Schleicher
Director for Education and Skills, Organisation for Economic
Co-operation and Development

'Macat is taking on some of the major challenges in university education … They have drawn together a strong team of active academics who are producing teaching materials that are novel in the breadth of their approach.'

Prof Lord Broers,
former Vice-Chancellor of the University of Cambridge

'The Macat vision is exceptionally exciting. It focuses upon new modes of learning which analyse and explain seminal texts which have profoundly influenced world thinking and so social and economic development. It promotes the kind of critical thinking which is essential for any society and economy. This is the learning of the future.'

Rt Hon Charles Clarke, former UK Secretary of State for Education

'The Macat analyses provide immediate access to the critical conversation surrounding the books that have shaped their respective discipline, which will make them an invaluable resource to all of those, students and teachers, working in the field.'

Professor William Tronzo, University of California at San Diego

WAYS IN TO THE TEXT

KEY POINTS

- Michael E. Porter is an American professor at Harvard Business School; born in 1947 in the US state of Michigan, he grew up around the world on account of his father's military career.

- In *Competitive Strategy* (1980), Porter identified five forces of competition* in an industry: suppliers* (providers of materials required by a business), buyers (customers), substitutes* (roughly, cheaper alternatives to a product or service), potential entrants (possible newcomers to a specific market), and industry rivals.

- Not only has Porter's book shaped the thinking of corporate leaders for 30 years, it has also attracted interest from academics and members of the wider public keen to understand how successful businesses behave.

Who Is Michael E. Porter?

The author of *Competitive Strategy: Techniques for Analyzing Industries and Competitors* (1980), Michael E. Porter, was born in 1947 in the city of Ann Arbor in the US state of Michigan. His father was a career army officer, and Michael grew up in a number of countries where his father served. He studied aerospace (aviation) and mechanical engineering at Princeton University, graduating first in his class in

1969. From there he went to Harvard University, where he earned an MBA with high distinction from the Harvard Business School in 1971, and a PhD in business economics in 1973.

Porter's research has focused on competitive strategy* (the means available to the business owner or organization seeking to increase the profitability or success of the business or organization over others) and competitiveness. His interest in this subject began with his experience in sports—as a high school student he was one of the top baseball and football players in his state, and as an undergraduate he was one of the top American university golfers.[1]

After earning his PhD, Porter remained in the academic world, lecturing at the Harvard Business School. In 1980, he published the first edition of *Competitive Strategy*. It quickly became an influential business text, and an international best seller; by 2016, it had been translated into 19 languages and had been reprinted 63 times. The text serves as part of the core curriculum at Harvard Business School, as well as at almost every business school in the world.

Since 2001, Porter has directed the Institute for Strategy and Competitiveness at Harvard Business School. He is one of the most cited academics in business and economics.[2]

His later publications have expanded on the ideas put forward in *Competitive Strategy*. They look at competitiveness at the level of the nation and the relationship between competition and society.

Porter has also served as a consultant to American politicians at various levels, to governments around the world, and to a good many companies looking to put the ideas in *Competitive Strategy* into action. He has also followed his lifelong love of sport by advising the Boston Red Sox baseball team on competitive strategy. As a consultant he has been generally successful, though in 2012 the consulting firm he cofounded, Monitor Group, went into bankruptcy. Porter lives in Brookline, Massachusetts.

What Does *Competitive Strategy* Say?

Competitive Strategy provides businesses with a strong framework for thinking about how to compete in their industries. This framework expands on a journal article Porter had written in the *Harvard Business Review* in 1979.[3]

In the first section of *Competitive Strategy*, Porter describes the five forces of competition: suppliers, buyers, substitute products, potential entrants, and industry rivals. This framework offers powerful tools for understanding a competitive environment.[4] His main aim in the text, however, was to answer the question of how companies might best succeed against their competitors.

Porter's answer is that they do this either by being more efficient and cheaper, or by being different, better, or more relevant. For Porter, these are the only two ways to succeed.

According to Porter it is not only a business's competitors who can have an effect on its performance; environmental factors are crucially important. Buyers, sellers, companies not yet in the industry (but who might enter it), and other products are also important. This was new thinking, going against what had been generally believed among business scholars at the time. Management writers before Porter had concentrated on areas he considered less important such as expanding market share.

The airline industry offers a useful example of Porter's ideas. For instance, the Irish airline Ryanair* has opted to compete in the market by using cost leadership*—structuring the business around low overhead costs and cheap prices. On the other hand, a company can charge more by providing services or technological innovation its competitors do not; Singapore Airlines, for example, was the first airline to offer individual television screens for passengers flying economy. Finally, a company can operate effectively if it can find a niche market, such as providing private jets.

While Porter did not invent these ideas about competing effectively by providing a cheaper or differentiated product, he certainly thought about them in new, thorough ways, and provided a framework that was easy to apply to a broad range of actual business scenarios. He built on nineteenth-century economic ideas of comparative advantage,* according to which a company—or a country—focuses on producing what it can make most cheaply and efficiently. He took those ideas and applied them in a new, clear way that makes sense with regard to modern business problems.

Competitive Strategy examines how to apply this framework to many different business sectors. For Porter, industries can be fragmented, with different firms serving different parts of the market (the low-price mass market, and the expensive high-end market in clothing, for example) and he examines strategies that businesses can follow in emerging, mature, and declining markets. If we assume printing to be in decline, for example, there may still be a market in this industry for high-end goods and services such as luxury craft bookbinding or letterpress (an old-fashioned printing technique in which letters are "set" with moveable blocks).

Porter's research has inspired many others to look into features of competition. He built on his own work in *Competitive Strategy* with his 1985 book *Competitive Advantage: Creating and Sustaining Superior Performance,* where he introduced new ideas like the value chain,* a way of looking at a business's production of goods or services by breaking it down into a number of separate steps.

Porter's clever understanding of five forces that broadly shape all kinds of business competition attracted many different readers, from economists to heads of corporations and the general public.

Why Does *Competitive Strategy* Matter?

Since its publication in 1980, *Competitive Strategy* has remained an important text. At business schools throughout the world, it has been used to train business leaders to understand competitive markets, and has been a basis of Harvard Business School's own course for new chief executives of Fortune 500* companies (the biggest American companies as compiled by the US magazine *Fortune*). It has been hailed as one of the most influential business and management books of the last four decades.[5]

The five-force analysis technique outlined in the work will help executives run their businesses with a clear strategic direction, prepared for the way their competitors are likely to act, and with a sound knowledge of how their industry is developing.

Business professionals using Porter's tools will be able to plan ahead as if they are playing chess, always thinking a few moves ahead of their opponents, rather than paying attention to short-term operational challenges only.

As well as providing general theories for analyzing competition, *Competitive Strategy* also provides businesses with concrete lessons. For example, companies that position themselves as a low-cost option in their industry protect themselves at once against all five of Porter's competitive forces. Firms that are neither the low-cost option, nor the differentiated one, can charge a premium, but can also be stuck in the middle, needing time and long effort to get out of a tricky position. Porter investigates this in what he calls the "hole in the middle problem."*

Competitive Strategy has received a number of prizes, including the Academy of Management's award for outstanding contribution to management thought. Four different "Porter prizes" have since been named after the author, awarded to companies that have applied his lessons in an exemplary way in their industry—in Japan (2001), India (2012), South Korea (2014) and, more generally, health care (2014).[6]

Decades after publication, *Competitive Strategy* is still required reading for anyone interested in understanding how companies form strategies about how best to compete. As the dean of the University of

Toronto's Rotman School of Business, Roger Martin,* noted, "Everyone who talks about sustainable competitive advantage* and how they're going to get it [uses business concepts originated by Porter's *Competitive Strategy*.]"[7]

NOTES

1   Walter Kiechel, *The Lords of Strategy: The Secret Intellectual History of the New Corporate World* (Cambridge, MA: Harvard Business Press, 2010).

2   Joan Magretta, *Understanding Michael Porter: The Essential Guide to Competition and Strategy* (Cambridge, MA: Harvard Business Review Press, 2011).

3   Michael E. Porter, "How Competitive Forces Shape Strategy," *Harvard Business Review* 57.2 (1979): 86–93.

4   Michael E. Porter, *Competitive Strategy: Techniques for Analyzing Industries and Competitors*, 2nd ed. (New York: Free Press, 1998).

5   Arthur Bedeian and Daniel Wren, "Most Influential Management Books of the 20th Century," *Organizational Dynamics* 29.3 (2001): 221–25.

6   The Porter Prize, "About," accessed January 29, 2016, http://www.porterprize.org/english/about/.

7   Geoff Colvin, "There's No Quit in Michael Porter," *Fortune Magazine*, October 15, 2012, accessed January 29, 2016, http://fortune.com/2012/10/15/theres-no-quit-in-michael-porter/.

SECTION 1
INFLUENCES

MODULE 1
THE AUTHOR AND THE
HISTORICAL CONTEXT

KEY POINTS

- *Competitive Strategy* introduced new ways of considering strategy—plans to achieve certain goals—and competition* in the business sector.

- Porter's childhood interest in competitive sport inspired his interest in strategic approaches to competition.

- In the years since *Competitive Strategy* was written, nearly every business school graduate has been exposed to the principles in Porter's book, giving it a tremendous influence on the business sector as a whole.

Why Read This Text?

Michael E. Porter's *Competitive Strategy: Techniques for Analyzing Industries and Competitors* (1980) is one of the most important texts in the field of business management and strategy. According to Joan Magretta,* a well-known former editor of the leading business magazine *Harvard Business Review,* Porter is "the most cited scholar in economics and business. At the same time, his ideas are the most widely used in practice by business and government leaders around the world. His frameworks have become the foundation of the strategy* field."[1]

Competitive Strategy introduces several key concepts, notably the five forces* of suppliers* (those who provide the resources and services a business requires), buyers (customers), substitutes* (less expensive replacements for a product or service), potential entrants (newcomers to a specific market), and industry rivals. Others were

❝ It is hard to concoct a logic in which the nature of the arena in which firms compete would not be important to performance outcomes. ❞

Michael E. Porter, *Competitive Strategy: Techniques for Analyzing Industries and Competitors*

competitive advantage* (qualities that allow an organization to outperform competitors), the value chain* (the various activities a business performs to produce a good or service), industry structure* (the nature of the business environment), and differentiation* (making a product different to others on the market).

Today, these ideas are used widely, but not always as Porter had intended—many refer to these concepts according to an inaccurate or incomplete understanding.[2] To understand the work's powerful insights and put them into practice requires that we are aware of and avoid frequent misunderstandings.

There is a misconception that competition is about being the best; for Porter, it is about being unique. Many wrongly think competition is a contest to the death between rivals—actually, it is strictly a battle over profits. And while many think strategy means being all things to all people, it requires, in fact, choices to make some customers happy.[3] The sign of a good strategy, according to Porter, is that it deliberately makes some customers unhappy.

Author's Life

Born in 1947 into an army family in Michigan, Porter travelled widely abroad throughout his childhood, experiencing different countries and cultures. On returning to the United States, he excelled in competitive sports—baseball, football, and golf—in both secondary school and university, which further increased his interest in competition and strategy.

Academically, he began as a student of engineering, graduating from Princeton University in 1969. He then adapted his technical and mathematical background to business and economics. Immediately after graduating, he went to Harvard University for a Master of Business Administration degree (MBA) and then moved on to the graduate school, where he completed a doctorate in business economics in 1973.

Porter is best known for work on competitiveness and strategy, which he brought together in his 1980 book *Competitive Strategy*. He first began exploring the ideas in the book in an academic article on the subject in the *Harvard Business Review*, published the year before.[4] He then continued to expand on the ideas in *Competitive Strategy* in other books, notably *Competitive Advantage: Creating and Sustaining Superior Performance* (1985). In total, he has written 19 books, and is widely considered the father of the modern strategy field.[5] He holds the chair of Bishop William Lawrence University Professor at the Harvard Business School, one of the 24 most senior professorial posts in the university.

In 2000, Harvard established an Institute for Strategy and Competitiveness, based in the Harvard Business School, whose website describes its mission as "extending the research pioneered by Porter and disseminating it to scholars and practitioners on a global basis."[6] The institute focuses on competition and its implications for company strategy; on the competitiveness of larger units than companies, such as nations, regions, and cities; and on the relationship between competition and society.

Author's Background

Porter's early work pioneered the use of economic theory to understand in a more thorough way the choices companies make to compete, and the dynamics of competition within an industry. The two most important themes in *Competitive Strategy* are industry structure (the make-up of the market place in terms of businesses, customers, products, and so on) and strategic positioning* (the means available to a business to place itself in the market in the most beneficial way). Along with his later idea of the value chain (the activities performed by a business as it brings a product to market) these remain central to Porter's work.

The 1980s in the United States were a time of both economic expansion and insecurity about the rise of competition from East Asian companies, especially from Japan. *Competitive Strategy* offered American businesses an intellectual framework for planning to compete with Japanese companies.

After writing *Competitive Strategy*, Porter further explored its ideas by turning to economic development and competitiveness on bigger scales—that is to say, he used microeconomic* factors (economics on a smaller scale—decisions of a single company, for example) to study the economic development of regions and nations. Here, he developed the idea of clusters* and created the Cluster Mapping Project,* which studies clusters of related business in US regions. He helped pioneer the field of economic geography*—a field that looks to map how transport costs and closeness to suppliers, personnel, and other businesses make some industries develop in some places quicker than in others.

Other areas in which Porter went on to apply the ideas in *Competitive Strategy* include health care and the role of corporations in society. His work—especially a 2011 article coauthored with the business strategist Mark Kramer,* "Creating Shared Value"[7]—has helped change the way companies approach corporate social responsibility;* Porter describes corporate social responsibility not as philanthropy (giving money to others), but as creating social value by, for example, locating business projects and enterprises in places that will help poor people.

Porter is also well known for the "Porter hypothesis,"* which holds that strict environmental standards could improve both company profits and national competitiveness by encouraging innovation and efficiency. This hypothesis has prompted several hundred academic articles by other scholars in the field of environmental economics.[8]

Indeed, a senior editor at *Fortune* magazine said of Porter: "He has influenced more executives—and more nations—than any other business professor on earth."[9]

NOTES

1   Joan Magretta, *Understanding Michael Porter: The Essential Guide to Competition and Strategy* (Cambridge, MA: Harvard Business Review Press, 2011).

2   See Magretta, *Understanding Michael Porter*, 121–40.

3   Magretta, *Understanding Michael Porter*, 111.

4   Michael E. Porter, "How Competitive Forces Shape Strategy," *Harvard Business Review* 57.2 (1979): 86–93.

5   Antonio Nieto-Rodriguez *The Focused Organization: How Concentrating on a Few Key Initiatives Can Dramatically Improve Strategy Execution* (Burlington, VT: Ashgate, 2012), 202.

6   Institute for Strategy and Competitiveness, "Home," accessed January 29, 2016, http://www.isc.hbs.edu/.

7   Michael E. Porter and Mark R. Kramer, "Creating Shared Value," *Harvard Business Review*, (2011): 63–70.

8   Google Scholar, "Porter Hypothesis," accessed January 29, 2016, https://scholar.google.com/scholar?hl=en&q=%22Porter+Hypothesis%22&btnG=&as_sdt=1%2C9&as_sdtp=.

9   Geoff Colvin, "There's No Quit in Michael Porter," *Fortune Magazine*, October 15, 2012, accessed January 29, 2016, http://fortune.com/2012/10/15/theres-no-quit-in-michael-porter/.

MODULE 2
ACADEMIC CONTEXT

KEY POINTS

- Strategy began with military campaigns and national government; it entered the business vocabulary after World War II* (1939–45).

- Academics including Kenneth Andrews* at the Harvard Business School adapted the concept of strategy to business so that it could be taught to business students.

- *Competitive Strategy* was written toward the end of a century that saw a number of great management experts who looked at different issues in running a successful company.

The Work in its Context

In *Competitive Strategy: Techniques for Analyzing Industries and Competitors*, Michael E. Porter describes strategy* as a "broad formula for how a business is going to compete, what its goals should be, and what policies will be needed to carry out those goals."[1] For him, it is the "combination of the ends (goals) for which the firm is striving and the means (policies) by which it is seeking to get there."[2]

One of Porter's key findings about business strategy is the claim that companies should specialize in a particular section of their market, rather than try to be all things to all people. This reflects ideas of comparative advantage* that trace back to the economist David Ricardo* in the nineteenth century. According to Ricardo, each country should practice extreme specialization in the industries in which it is most competitive. For example, member nations of the Organization of Petroleum Exporting Countries* (OPEC)

> **❝** A number of other books about competition have come and gone because they were really about special cases, or were grounded not in the principles of competitive strategy but in particular competitive practices. **❞**
>
> Michael E. Porter, *Competitive Strategy: Techniques for Analyzing Industries and Competitors*

specialize in crude oil production, and Canada specializes in maple syrup (among many other products).

Producing any products other than the ones that it can produce at the lowest marginal cost* ("products A") means a country must pay the opportunity cost* of producing other commodities ("products B"), when it could have been producing products A instead. "Marginal cost" here is the extra cost of producing one more unit; "opportunity cost" is the value of the best alternative action to the one actually taken.

If a country uses its resources to produce more of product A, it can sell the excess and use the revenue to buy product B from a nation that can produce product B most efficiently. For example, Iceland has a large and efficient fisheries industry. It exports large quantities of cod and uses the earnings to buy many things it cannot produce efficiently, such as bananas. This is a wise choice, since if Iceland decided instead to take some investment capital and workers away from the fisheries to build and use expensive heated hot houses to grow bananas, it would end up with fewer cod to sell and fewer bananas to eat.

Ricardo's work on comparative advantage is actually the basis for the widespread present-day agreement in favor of free trade. If each country focuses on producing products that it makes best, by selling those products to other countries it can generate income with which to purchase items that it is less efficient at producing—and at a greater volume than it could have made on its own.

In *Competitive Strategy*, Porter argues that companies should focus sharply on a particular niche, like resource extraction (mining minerals or extracting oil, for example), manufacturing certain goods, or providing certain services.

Overview of the Field

The notion of strategy has been around since perhaps even the dawn of nation states. Leaders use strategies (the plan) and tactics (the maneuvers) to ensure victory over an opponent. The term derives from the Greek word for generalship, *stratēgia*. A *stratēgos* is a general, and this was the title of the fourth-century B.C.E. military leader and conqueror Alexander the Great* and his father, Philip II of Macedon.* Over time, the field of strategic studies has grown up. This includes military strategy and business strategy and any other field where there is a degree of competition.*

However, the shift from military to business strategy did not take place until after World War II. The business strategist Kenneth Andrews played a key role. In 1946, he joined the Harvard Business School faculty after earning a doctorate on the famous American writer Mark Twain* and serving in the army during the war. In 1950, he and several colleagues began revising the school's business policy course. After two years, they selected the concept of corporate strategy as the course's organizing principle.

Andrews began writing case studies (studies of real-life examples) from the point of view of senior management, specifically addressing all of the challenges facing a company such as the identification of threats and opportunities, and understanding what the company stands for. The course produced two important books: *Business Policy: Text and Cases* (1965), and *The Concept of Corporate Strategy* (1971).[3]

In Andrews's early formulation of business strategy, strategy was deliberate—consciously decided and adopted by management. His principles included that strategies must have an ethical component, and that they must be in agreement with the values of the upper managers.

A different view was advanced by Henry Mintzberg,* a Canadian academic business strategist for whom the approach was undemocratic and too "top-down" (that is, focused on management). He instead emphasized the importance of what he called "emergent strategy"*—strategy that emerges informally at any level in an organization. It is an alternative to, or a supplement for, the deliberate strategy determined by, or with the agreement of, senior management.

Academic Influences

By the time Porter had developed the ideas in *Competitive Strategy*, the book included ideas contributed by other colleagues, too. The business historian Alfred DuPont Chandler,* who came to the Harvard Business School in 1970, received a Pulitzer prize (a prestigious literary prize) in 1977 for his book *The Visible Hand: The Managerial Revolution in American Business*.[4] Chandler's book formed part of a "managerial revolution"* that looked at the importance of managers in organizing and running large businesses.

Chandler had also written an earlier book, *Strategy and Structure: Chapters in the History of the American Industrial Enterprise* (1962), which looked at large American businesses, tracing how each company's business strategy determined how the company was structured.[5] Chandler summarized his argument with the phrase "Structure follows strategy."[6]

Other academics promptly turned this around, suggesting strategy follows structure. A multidivision structure (in which a company is divided into different divisions strongly separated from one another), for example, leads a business to adopt a conglomerate strategy,*[7] in which it adds new goods or services to diversify into different markets unrelated to its current business.

It is worth placing *Competitive Strategy* in context alongside the other chief management books of the twentieth century. The first and most influential remains the early management scholar Frederick Winslow Taylor's* *The Principles of Scientific Management* (1911).[8] Taylor advocated running a business in the most efficient way with workplace tasks standardized so that they might be performed in the shortest amount of time. The book led to the start of management as a discipline.

The business scholar Chester Barnard's* *The Functions of the Executive* (1938),[9] was the next, and one of the first books to consider leadership from a social and psychological viewpoint (that is, considering the role of the human mind in behavior). Herbert Simon's* suitably titled *Administrative Behavior: A Study of Decision-Making Processes in Administrative Organizations* (1947) remains one of the most cited management works in social science.[10]

A skeptical note came in with the influential management scholars Paul Lawrence* and Jay Lorsch's* *Organization and Environment*[11] in 1967, which questioned whether there was a single best way to organize, independent of the details of the industry, market, or overall business environment. Lawrence and Lorsch did not believe there was, and instead introduced the concept of contingency,* according to which ideal leadership differs based on the task and environment.

Competitive Strategy draws on a tradition of business strategy that had begun to flourish at the Harvard Business School in the years before Porter began working there. However, where earlier writers focused on ethics or efficiency, Porter turns the discussion about strategy to the conflict of companies with one another in the marketplace.

NOTES

1   Michael E. Porter, *Competitive Strategy: Techniques for Analyzing Industries and Competitors*, 2nd ed. (New York: Free Press, 1998), xxiv.

2   Porter, *Competitive Strategy*, xxiv.

3   Philip Learned et al., *Business Policy: Text and Cases* (Homewood, IL: R. D. Irwin, 1969); and Kenneth R. Andrews, *The Concept of Corporate Strategy* (Homewood, IL: R. D. Irwin, 1994).

4   Alfred Chandler, *The Visible Hand: The Managerial Revolution in American Business* (Cambridge, MA: Belknap Press, 1977).

5   Alfred Chandler, *Strategy and Structure: Chapters in the History of the American Industrial Enterprise* (Cambridge, MA: MIT Press, 1962).

6   Chandler, *Strategy and Structure*, 14.

7   David Hall and Maurice Saias, "Strategy Follows Structure!" *Strategic Management Journal* 1.2 (1980): 149–63.

8   Frederick Winslow Taylor, *The Principles of Scientific Management* (New York: Harper Brothers, 1911).

9   Chester Barnard, *The Functions of the Executive* (Cambridge, MA: Harvard University Press, 1938).

10 Herbert Simon, *Administrative Behavior: A Study of Decision-Making Processes in Administrative Organizations* (New York: Macmillan, 1947).

11 Paul Lawrence and Jay Lorsch, *Organization and Environment* (Boston, MA: Harvard Business School, Division of Research,1967).

MODULE 3
THE PROBLEM

KEY POINTS

- Through the mid-1950s, companies focused on increasing production to increase profit; with growing consumer choice, however, Porter proposed instead a focus on better satisfying consumers in a section of the market.

- As Porter developed his ideas in the 1970s, he drew on several leading, competing, models of business strategy.

- Finding problems with all the leading models, Porter ended up drawing most from the economist Joe Bain's* structure-conduct-performance* model, which looks at how market structure affects a business's performance.

Core Question

In *Competitive Strategy: Techniques for Analyzing Industries and Competitors*, Michael E. Porter asks how companies can best find profitable industries to compete in, and, having found an attractive industry, what strategy they should adopt to compete most effectively.

He poses the question of how companies should make important choices about the scope and type of competitive advantage*— qualities that permit an organization to outperform competitors— they seek in their industries. According to earlier studies, business strategies should simply be aimed at selling the highest volume of products possible.[1] Porter found this answer unsatisfying; more, it was not in keeping with empirical (real-world) research into which companies made the largest profits and competed most effectively.

Throughout the mid-1950s, a production orientation* strategy was most common in industry; this presumed that if a company

> ❝ The essence of formulating competitive strategy
> is relating a company to its environment … [The]
> key aspect of the firm's environment is the industry
> or industries in which it competes. The intensity of
> competition in an industry is neither a matter of
> coincidence nor bad luck. Rather, competition in an
> industry is rooted in its underlying economic structure
> and goes well beyond the behavior of current
> competitors. ❞
>
> Michael E. Porter, *Competitive Strategy: Techniques for Analyzing Industries and Competitors*

created a long-lasting product of high technical quality that worked well, it would return a profit.

The Harvard Business School professor Theodore Levitt* helped replace this production orientation model in an important 1960 *Harvard Business Review* article called "Marketing Myopia."* He called on companies to switch to a consumer orientation by working to meet customers' needs, rather than start with a superior product and then think of how to sell it.[2]

A perfect example of this is when Henry Ford,* the founder of the Ford Motor Company, mockingly said customers could have a Model T (the first mass-produced, and relatively affordable car) in any color they liked, so long as it was black.[3] At the time of his comment, however, there had been a shortage of consumer goods that would worsen during the catastrophic economic downturn of the late 1920s and 1930s, known as the Great Depression,* and World War II* (1939–45), which meant that businesses only needed to produce a technically superb product to find a market.

Levitt's new consumer orientation model appeared to be better suited to an era of economic growth, when a growing supply of consumer goods was available. However, this model required the adoption of a new set of tools that business leaders could use to make strategic business decisions that took into account broader issues, like rival producers and customers faced with a variety of choices. It is these tools that Porter tries to provide in *Competitive Strategy*.

The Participants

A scholar who made a significant contribution to this debate was Albert Humphrey* of Stanford Research International,* a research institute of Stanford University in California, who in the 1960s and 1970s helped popularize the so-called SWOT analysis,* studying Strengths, Weaknesses, Opportunities, and Threats, to help a business against its competitors. Humphrey considered a business to have a strategic fit*—a suitable place in the market—if its resources and capabilities matched with opportunities in its external environment.

A second important scholar was Bruce Henderson,* founder of the Boston Consulting Group,* a leading management consulting firm. Beginning in 1968, he began drawing lessons for strategy from what scholars call the "experience curve."* This curve reflects the idea that the more often you do something, the more easily and efficiently you can do it again. It was first measured in 1936 at Wright-Patterson Air Force Base* in Dayton, Ohio, where it was recognized that when work on aircraft doubled, the required labor time decreased 10–15 percent; in other industries, this was as high as 30 percent.

Henderson concluded that a lower cost of operations gives a company an important advantage over competitors. Therefore, businesses should focus on getting enough market share*—the percentage of a market accounted for by a particular business—to take advantage of the experience curve. For Henderson, producing more of an item gives employees more experience in producing it—and an advantage over rivals.

A third key scholar was Joe Bain, an important figure in industrial organization economics.* Bain focused not on businesses or the economy as a whole, but on a particular industry. Looking into questions such as barriers to entering a specific industry, he developed what was called the structure-conduct-performance paradigm, which considers how market structure—the "environment" of competition, customer base, products, and so on—affects a business's performance .[4]

A fourth scholar, who like Bain had an important influence on Porter, was Alfred DuPont Chandler,* a colleague at the Harvard Business School who won a Pulitzer prize for his book *The Visible Hand: The Managerial Revolution in American Business* three years before Porter's *Competitive Strategy* was published.

The Contemporary Debate

Before *Competitive Strategy* appeared, the leading view in business strategy was derived from the analysis of Bruce Henderson; companies were encouraged to try to gain the highest market share to take advantage of the experience curve.

But this approach found challenges. In the late 1960s, the marketing analyst Sidney Schoeffler* of the US business giant General Electric* began a large research project, the Profit Impact of Marketing Strategy (PIMS),* which collected observations from 2,600 business units in 200 companies between 1970 and 1983. In contrast to Henderson's views on strategy, not only were firms with a high market share often very profitable, so were firms with *low* market share. The least profitable firms fell in the middle, with moderate market share—a "hole in the middle"* problem.[5] Porter also found that Henderson's SWOT analysis was not sufficiently thorough; he turned instead to the recent work of the economist Joe Bain for a model.

Bain's structure-conduct-performance model (on which Porter bases his own five forces)* looks for relationships between the structure of a market and an industry's performance. In particular, it looks for connections between how businesses behave in an industry, and the structure of the surrounding market—the barriers to new companies entering, how different are the products of different companies, and the degree to which supply and demand is concentrated in a particular region or section of the population.

Also at around this time, Chandler's *Visible Hand* had drawn great attention to the importance of a team of managers in organizing complex modern businesses.[6] But Chandler's book was a work of economic history rather than business strategy, and it reinforced in the public mind—and in Porter's—the importance of providing career business administrators with professional technical skills for their job.

NOTES

1   *The Economist* editors, "The Experience Curve," *The Economist*, September 14, 2009, accessed February 8, 2016, http://www.economist.com/node/14298944.

2   Theodore Levitt, "Marketing Myopia," *Harvard Business Review* (1960): 45–56.

3   Henry Ford with Samuel Crowther, *My Life and Work* (Garden City, NY: Doubleday, Page, 1923), 72.

4   Joseph S. Bain, *Industrial Organization* (New York: John Wiley & Sons, 1959).

5   Michael E. Porter, *Competitive Strategy: Techniques for Analyzing Industries and Competitors*, 2nd ed. (New York: Free Press, 1998), 42.

6   Alfred Chandler, *The Visible Hand: The Managerial Revolution in American Business* (Cambridge, MA: Belknap Press, 1977).

MODULE 4
THE AUTHOR'S CONTRIBUTION

KEY POINTS

- In *Competitive Strategy*, Porter offers a model of competitive forces in an industry and how these forces affected the profitability of businesses competing in it.

- Porter's five forces* include three "horizontal" forces (established rivals, new entrants, and the threat of substitute products) and two "vertical" forces (the bargaining power of suppliers,* on one side, and consumers on the other).

- Other strategy planning tools for businesses include Bruce Henderson's* somewhat superseded growth-share matrix,* focusing on market share, and the political, economic, social, and technological PEST analysis,* often seen today along with Porter's five forces.

Author's Aims

In *Competitive Strategy: Techniques for Analyzing Industries and Competitors*, Michael E. Porter tries to use recent research to take a broader view of all the forces impacting on a business. As Porter says, "competition* in an industry goes well beyond the established players. Customers, suppliers, substitutes,* and potential entrants are all 'competitors' to firms in the industry and may be more or less prominent depending on the particular circumstances."[1]

By using a framework that takes each of these into account, managers and strategists can make better-informed decisions about which markets to compete in, and how to go about it.

Porter published *Competitive Strategy* in 1980. He had been lecturing at the Harvard Business School since completing his doctorate in business

> **❝** The collective strength of these [five basic competitive] forces determines the ultimate profit potential in the industry, where profit potential is measured in terms of long run return on invested capital. Not all industries have the same potential. **❞**
>
> Michael E. Porter, *Competitive Strategy: Techniques for Analyzing Industries and Competitors*

economics in 1973. He was influenced by coursework in industrial organization economics* (inquiry into the structure of firms and markets) that he took there as a student. This coursework attempted to model how competitive forces affected industries and how profitable the industries were in different circumstances.

During the 1960s and 1970s, researchers at the Harvard Business School such as Kenneth Andrews* and Alfred DuPont Chandler* had been looking into the drivers of profitability. The research had led these and other scholars to become particularly interested in the problems of strategy and the role of senior managers.

Yet two leading approaches to analyzing problems of strategy for managers—the Strengths, Weaknesses, Opportunities, and Threats (SWOT) analysis* and the experience curve,* founded on the observation that the more times a task has been performed, the less time is required to perform it again—struck Porter as flawed. The SWOT analysis, though still frequently used today, was not based on any thorough research or theory, and the experience curve did not explain how businesses with a small market share* (a percentage of the market) could be equally profitable to ones with very large shares.

Approach

Porter's five forces* sum up how competitive and attractive an industry is by looking at what affects the ability of a business in that industry to make a profit.

The five forces Porter identified are:
- the bargaining power of suppliers (those who supply things such as materials to a business)
- the threat of established rivals
- the threat of new entrants (newcomers to a market)
- the bargaining power of buyers (that is, roughly, consumer choice)
- the threat of substitution.

A business within an industry can then make profits that are more or less than the industry average by coming up with a business model that is better or worse than its competitors.

Porter also tackles the hole in the middle problem*—why, in the experience curve model, firms with very small or very large market share are successful, while ones in the middle are less profitable.

Porter argues that high market-share businesses follow a strategy of cost leadership:* using mass production* (mechanized production on a large scale) and taking advantage of economies of scale* (the fact that it is cheaper, per unit, to produce goods in greater quantities), they are able to offer a product more cheaply than their competitors. Small market-share businesses instead successfully use a strategy of market segmentation:* they correctly identify a niche in the market that is small but profitable.

Firms with a market share in the middle, on the other hand, are less likely to be able to compete with larger firms on cost, or with smaller firms in satisfying the needs of a niche. They are the least profitable as a result.

Contribution in Context
The five-forces approach Porter outlined in *Competitive Strategy* is one of several widely used analyses for understanding how to compete within a given industry.

An older approach, developed by Bruce Henderson* at the Boston Consulting Group* in 1970, is called the growth-share matrix.* Also known as "the product portfolio" or "portfolio planning analysis," it ranks business units or products based on their market share and growth rate. "Cash cows" have high market share in a slow-growing industry (and are to be milked, with low investment), whereas "dogs" have low market share in a slow-growing industry (and are to be sold off). "Stars" command high market share in a fast-growing industry, and require high funding to fight off competition, while "question marks" have low market share in a high-growth market, and will evolve into one of the other three.

One drawback of this approach is that it charts market share and an industry's growth rate, and only *suggests* profitability—the actual purpose of any business. Moreover, research has shown that businesses using this approach had lower shareholder returns than ones that did not.[2] Many business textbooks have begun removing the growth-share matrix.

Another framework for strategic analysis in looking at different factors in a company's environment is the PEST analysis, named for its analysis of political, economic, social, and technological factors. Political factors include tax policy; economic factors include interest rates; social factors include how quickly consumers within an economy are aging; technological factors include the rate of technological change. It should be noted that there are variants of this; with legal factors included, it is known as the "SLEPT" analysis; with environmental and legal factors it becomes a "PESTLE" framework.

NOTES

1 Michael E. Porter, *Competitive Strategy: Techniques for Analyzing Industries and Competitors*, 2nd ed. (New York: Free Press, 1998), 6.

2 Stanley Slater and Thomas Zwirlein, "Shareholder Value and Investment Strategy Using the General Portfolio Model," *Journal of Management* 18.4 (1992): 717–32.

SECTION 2
IDEAS

MODULE 5
MAIN IDEAS

KEY POINTS

- Porter says businesses should look at five key issues in their particular industry: the threat of new entrants; the threat of substitute products; the power of buyers; the power of suppliers;* industry rivals.

- For Porter, who looks at each of these competitive forces in detail, strategy is principally a question of building and sustaining competitive advantage.*

- The language used by Porter in *Competitive Strategy* is directed at business practitioners, and is remarkably free of jargon, academic language, or mathematics.

Key Themes

The core themes of Michael E. Porter's *Competitive Strategy: Techniques for Analyzing Industries and Competitors* are the effects on competition* of new entrants, substitute products, buyer power, supplier power, and the intensity of industry rivalry.

New entrants are businesses that are not currently present in a sector. However, they may see profitable markets, and will tend to enter them until—due to the increased competition—the profitability has decreased for all businesses in the sector.

Substitute products are goods that a consumer sees as similar or comparable. While, for the beverage producer Coke, Pepsi is a competitor for shares in the soft-drink market, the soft-drink market itself grows or shrinks as people choose instead to drink coffee drinks, energy drinks, alcoholic beverages, or sparkling water. These are substitute products.

> ❝ The goal of competitive strategy for a business unit in an industry is to find a position in the industry where the company can best defend itself against these competitive forces or can influence them in its favor. Since the collective strength of the forces may well be painfully apparent to all competitors, the key for developing strategy is to delve below the surface and analyze the sources of each. ❞
>
> Michael E. Porter, *Competitive Strategy: Techniques for Analyzing Industries and Competitors*

Buyer power is the bargaining ability of customers. It is high if buyers have many alternatives, or if there are only a few large buyers, or if buyers organize together to bargain. On the other hand, it is low if a large number of small buyers act independently of each other. An example of strong buyer power is Groupon, an online business that negotiates deals with other businesses for lower prices for Groupon clients, because of their large numbers. An extreme case is monopsony*—a situation where there is only one buyer in a market. The National Health Service in the United Kingdom is close to this, being practically the sole purchaser of hospital equipment in the country, and so can negotiate better deals. This is unlike in the United States, where each hospital has to purchase equipment independently.

Supplier power is closely related, and is the bargaining power of companies selling the materials and equipment that other producers need. An example of high supplier power is if a company bakes bread and there is only one firm selling flour—the company has no choice but to buy it. If there are many suppliers of flour, the baking business can hold out for a lower price.

Finally, industry rivalry reflects how aggressively competitors in a sector apply pressure to one another, and attempt to steal other businesses' market share and profits. Rivalry is high if there are many competitors, if they are of comparable market share, if brand loyalty is low, and if their products are undifferentiated (that is, can easily be substituted for one another). If an industry is growing quickly, or if the switching costs* to customers are high (that is, if it is costly for customers to switch to another producer, perhaps because customers have already invested in equipment to use the original product, and the equipment cannot be used for a competitor's product), then the industry rivalry may be low.

Exploring the Ideas

Porter deals with each of the competitive forces one by one. "New entrants to an industry," writes Porter, "bring new capacity, the desire to gain market share, and often substantial resources."[1] Therefore they can bid down prices, and reduce profitability for businesses already in the sector. On the other hand, Porter believes that outside firms could be discouraged from entering a sector by the economies of scale* (the lower cost per item that often comes from producing a large quantity of that item) enjoyed by companies that already have more market share, or the need to differentiate themselves, "forcing entrants," in Porter's words, "to spend heavily to overcome existing customer loyalties," which "usually involves start-up losses and often takes an extended period of time."[2]

Second is the threat of substitute products. Porter argues they "limit the potential returns of an industry by placing a ceiling on the prices firms in the industry can profitably charge."[3] For example, sugar producers may find a lid set on their profits by a low price for high fructose corn syrup, a substitute for sugar. Other forces, like switching costs (moving from one product to another), may help reduce the threat.

Third is buyers' bargaining power. Companies in an industry do not only compete with each other—they also compete with buyers, by "forcing down prices, bargaining for higher quality or more services, and playing competitors against each other—all at the expense of industry profitability," Porter notes.[4] One strategic decision, therefore, is which buyers a company chooses to sell to. "A company can improve its strategic posture by finding buyers who possess the least power to influence it adversely," Porter says.[5]

The fourth is supplier power. Suppliers can threaten to raise prices or reduce the quality of the goods or services they offer. An industry unable to pass on price increases to customers will see its profitability squeezed out. Labor, for Porter, is a supplier: "Highly skilled employees and/or tightly unionized labor [workers organized with the aim of protecting things such as pay and working conditions] can bargain away a significant fraction of potential profits."[6]

The final factor in Porter's framework is industry rivalry; as he notes, "some forms of competition, notably price competition, are highly unstable and quite likely to leave the entire industry worse off from the standpoint of profitability."[7] One measure of rivalry is in advertising spending. For example, the advertisements of Apple, the highly successful manufacturer of computers and iPhones, often targeted its rival, Microsoft, the software company that controls a large part of the market for software for personal computers. In the ads, Apple portrayed itself as a young, hip person, whereas Microsoft was a middle-aged "nerd." Another is how much money competitive businesses in a sector are investing in developing new technology.

Rivalry is highest in markets in which sales are not growing or products are undifferentiated—they are very similar to one another. Porter says companies could try to change these conditions. "Focusing selling efforts on the fastest growing segments of the industry … can reduce the impact of industry rivalry," Porter observes.[8] Finding a way to escape market rivalry allows businesses to be more profitable.

Language and Expression

Porter makes clear in *Competitive Strategy* that he is writing for practitioners (that is, those actively involved in managing businesses or advising the people who are). As such, he sees his work as creating a bridge between scholars who do pure research and people occupied with the cut and thrust of business competition. As such, he was reaching across the chasm between actual business and stylized models from the world of theory.

As well as affecting his language (which is easily understood by anyone, and avoids mathematics or technical terms used in academic economics), his approach affected the work's focus. For Porter, writing for practitioners and in a language accessible to anyone meant he could examine issues that academic work had neglected. Academic economists, he argues, had been focusing mainly on industries, considering individual companies as equal in highly abstract models. Similarly, managers were absent in academic models.

This approach extends to the questions Porter addresses in *Competitive Strategy*: what the nature of competition in an industry means for company behavior, how to push profits up (a concern for businesses) rather than down (a concern for society, government policy, and for consumers), and how to understand competition among a small number of companies whose behavior affects each other.

NOTES

1 Michael E. Porter, *Competitive Strategy*, 2nd ed. (New York: Free Press, 1998), 7.

2 Porter, *Competitive Strategy*, 9.

3 Porter, *Competitive Strategy*, 23.

4 Porter, *Competitive Strategy*, 24.

5 Porter, *Competitive Strategy*, 26.

6 Porter, *Competitive Strategy*, 28.

7 Porter, *Competitive Strategy*, 17.

8 Porter, *Competitive Strategy*, 22.

MODULE 6
SECONDARY IDEAS

KEY POINTS

- After looking at the five forces,* *Competitive Strategy* looks at three approaches that Porter calls generic strategies;* these help businesses decide how to position themselves in their market.

- The three strategies are: offering the lowest prices; offering a differentiated product; focusing strongly on a niche market.

- Porter also provides analyses and strategies for overlooked but potentially profitable niches, including businesses in declining markets and businesses in rapidly globalizing* industries (industries increasingly operating across continental borders).

Other Ideas

The secondary themes of Michael E. Porter's *Competitive Strategy: Techniques for Analyzing Industries and Competitors* are how businesses can pursue a competitive advantage* by aiming at lower cost, a differentiated product, or a narrow focus on a target audience.

Lower cost—which he refers to as cost leadership*—aims at attracting the most price-sensitive customers. They will often have little brand loyalty, and will be easily targeted by competitors who can manage a still lower price.

Differentiation* (making a company's product different from similar products sold by other companies) is aimed at less price-sensitive customers who are not being served well by the existing market. It tends to be done best by larger companies.

❝ Effectively implementing any of these generic strategies usually requires total commitment and supporting organizational arrangements that are diluted if there is more than one primary target. **❞**

Michael E. Porter, *Competitive Strategy: Techniques for Analyzing Industries and Competitors*

Smaller companies are better suited to a niche strategy—identifying a narrower target market, and looking closely at its distinct needs.

These three approaches, which Porter calls "generic strategies," should be used alongside looking to his five forces to see where a company's competitive position is weakest. Alternatively, a company can try to reshape the five forces by differentiation—that is, trying to make its product different from that of its competitors. Or it can invest to erect entry barriers to dissuade new competitors, such as patents on new technologies (legal protections against their being copied), or spending heavily on new facilities. Through this process, called positioning,* a company adapts to the competitive environment around it.

The idea that a business can choose its strategy in this way was introduced by *Competitive Strategy*. Until this point, following the writings of the influential strategist Bruce Henderson* and the broad acceptance of the experience curve,* the general belief had been that there was precisely one strategy for all companies to follow—pursuing more market share.

Porter's important innovation was to point out that profitability, not market share, is the real goal for a business to pursue—and small businesses may also be very profitable. This means there are different approaches a company can employ.

Exploring the Ideas

According to Porter, cost leadership (offering the lowest prices) "requires aggressive construction of efficient-scale facilities, vigorous pursuit of cost reductions from experience, tight cost and overhead control, avoidance of marginal customer accounts, and cost minimization in areas like [research and development], service, sales force, [and] advertising."[1] Having a lower cost relative to competitors, he adds, "becomes the theme running through the entire strategy."[2]

It is helpful for this strategy if a company can have a high relative market share. Achieving this might require start-up losses, says Porter, such as heavy investment in state-of-the-art equipment, or favorable access to raw materials.

The strategy is a particularly appealing one, according to Porter, because it "protects the firm against all five competitive forces."[3] Bargaining with buyers and suppliers will "only continue to erode profits until those of the next efficient competitor are eliminated." In this process the less efficient competitors "will suffer first" in the face of competitive pressures.[4]

A business might attract price-sensitive customers by having the lowest prices, or the lowest ratio of price to value. A company might try to use its assets better than its competitors (an airline could turn around its flights more quickly; a restaurant could more quickly clear tables to allow the next guests to sit down). Costs of equipment or fixed costs, such as rent, staffing, or lighting, are known as sunk (that is, already paid-for) costs. If more product can be squeezed out, then these costs can then be divided over more units of product.

Another approach is for a company to market itself by offering standardized, no-frills products to purchasers, like the Irish low-cost airline Ryanair.* A downside to the strategy includes lower customer loyalty, because price-sensitive customers will switch when a similar—if slightly better—option becomes available.

Porter's second strategy—differentiation—may suit larger companies better. It targets customers who are slightly less price-sensitive, and are underserved by the existing market. It creates "something that is perceived *industry-wide* as being unique."[5] A company choosing this strategy should try to avoid a product that could easily be copied by competitors. It could do this by having unique technical skills, especially trained staff, or patents for new technologies.

Possible approaches to differentiating can take many forms, particularly good design or top-of-the-line brand image (the German luxury car manufacturer Mercedes Benz, for example).[6] Another approach might be excellent customer service or a reliable dealer network. Porter uses the US construction machinery company Caterpillar Inc. as an example, because it is "known not only for its dealer network and excellent spare parts availability but also for its extremely high-quality durable products."[7] However, Porter adds, "It should be stressed that the differentiation strategy does not allow the firm to ignore costs, but rather that they are not the primary strategic target."[8]

Finally, Porter's niche strategy—he also calls this "focus"—could work best for smaller businesses. Smaller groups of target clients might not provide enough volume for larger companies to recoup their investments in fixed costs. A target market might be geographic, it might be demographic (that is, a specific section of a population, such as a particular age bracket or ethnic group), or it might have to do with lifestyles.[9]

This strategy involves looking closely at the needs of a distinct group and its specialized needs. "The entire focus strategy is built around serving a particular target very well," he says.[10] This strategy hopes to generate a high degree of product loyalty. Competitive advantage in this case comes from innovation and brand marketing, not from the same strict attention to efficiency as the cost leadership strategy.

Porter observes that this focus (that is, niche) strategy is linked to the other two. "Even though the focus strategy does not achieve low cost or differentiation from the perspective of the market as a whole, it does achieve one or both of these positions vis-à-vis its narrow market target."[11]

Overlooked

Competitive Strategy is chiefly known for introducing Porter's five competitive forces, and his three generic strategies for responding to these forces.

Porter does, however, provide many other helpful insights into competing in particular types of industries. Chapter 12 of the book, for example, looks at declining industries, like cigar manufacture or bookbinding, while chapter 13 looks at industries undergoing rapid globalization, like the automotive industry at present. Neither of these two examples is frequently cited by other writers or practitioners— certainly not as often as the five forces and three generic strategies, which are referred to (if not always quite correctly) by business executives and consultants the world over. But both contain powerful observations.

For example, Porter observes that the common wisdom is that owners of businesses in declining industries* (industries experiencing a decline in demand) should stop making any new investments, generate as much cash flow as possible, and eventually divest (sell off the business). However, Porter points out that declining industries vary greatly, and some businesses have even done well with heavy new investment. To devise a successful strategy it is necessary to look at remaining pockets of demand—cigars, for instance, are in decline, but the premium segment (high-end cigars) remains. This market segment is price-insensitive and is open to high levels of new product differentiation. There are also buyers in some declining industries who might have to pay costly switching costs (the price of new equipment or training) to begin using another product, such as another computer system.

With globalization, Porter notes, producing for a global market can allow faster learning, and permit larger economies of scale*—the greater the number a product is manufactured in, the cheaper each unit is to manufacture. If underserved market segments exist in many countries, a company can try to serve the same niche in several countries at the same time. The market, for example, for "fair trade" mobile telephones (equipment built according to strict ethical and environmental standards) may in any single country be small, but worldwide may be enough for a company to begin benefiting from economies of scale.

NOTES

1   Michael E. Porter, *Competitive Strategy: Techniques for Analyzing Industries and Competitors*, 2nd ed. (New York: Free Press, 1998), 35.

2   Porter, *Competitive Strategy*, 35.

3   Porter, *Competitive Strategy*, 36.

4   Porter, *Competitive Strategy*, 36.

5   Porter, *Competitive Strategy*, 37.

6   Porter, *Competitive Strategy*, 37.

7   Porter, *Competitive Strategy*, 37.

8   Porter, *Competitive Strategy*, 37.

9   Porter, *Competitive Strategy*, 37.

10 Porter, *Competitive Strategy*, 38.

11 Porter, *Competitive Strategy*, 38–39.

MODULE 7
ACHIEVEMENT

KEY POINTS

- Porter's contribution is located between the rich detail of a business school case study and the highly abstract models of academic economics; he calls this level a "middle-ground framework."

- Part of the book's strength is derived from its stitching together of the fields of industrial organization economics* (inquiry into the structures of firms and markets) and business policy (strategy);* while both look at business behavior, they do not normally engage with each other.

- Limitations include the fact that, as a middle-level analysis, the book does not take into account contexts that are microeconomic* (inside the firm) or macroeconomic* (in the broader economy); he remedies this in his next book, *Competitive Advantage: Creating and Sustaining Superior Performance.*

Assessing the Argument.

To understand competitive forces, Michael E. Porter's *Competitive Strategy: Techniques for Analyzing Industries and Competitors* offers a "middle-ground framework"—a model more generalized than a case study of one company or industry, yet more detailed than an economic model.

As Porter notes, "The essence of formulating competitive strategy is relating the company to its environment."[1] *Competitive Strategy* stresses the idea of strategic choice by a company. A company achieves this through positioning (a strategic consideration of its products' place in the market) and through profitability.

❝ The chapter on generic strategies was the last chapter to be written. Again, it involved uncomfortable territory. Business school colleagues were saying, 'Too abstract' and 'We can't generalize,' while the economists were saying, 'Where are the statistical tests? What is the model?' It was a very uncomfortable leap. **❞**

Nicholas Argyres and Anita McGahan, "An Interview with Michael Porter," *The Academy of Management Executive*

It is worth noting that Porter's five forces* and three generic strategies* used in the process of positioning (cost, differentiation, focus on a section of the market) follow neither the case-study approach of business schools, nor the modeling approach from economics. Instead they offer what Porter calls "frameworks." As Porter explains, "a framework tries to capture the full richness of a phenomenon with the most limited number of dimensions."[2]

Porter's frameworks occupy a midway point between case studies and models, providing (Porter claims) the smallest number of "core elements that still capture the variation and dimensionality of competition."*[3] A framework's dimensions need to be intuitively grounded, and must make sense to a practitioner (a person running or advising a business). If it fails to do this, a framework will only serve to showcase the education, and justify the invoices, of a professional consultant class.

Achievement in Context

The early 1980s, when Porter published *Competitive Strategy,* was a critical juncture in the field of business strategy. The young field was rich in interesting questions, but poor in frameworks to analyze them.[4]

The field had seen promising work in the 1960s and early 1970s. But then in the later 1970s it was neglected when promised successes did not materialize. The big success at the time of Japanese companies, especially automakers, "did not seem to depend on planning as much as it did on quality, corporate and national culture, and management itself,"[5] in the words of one commentator. *Competitive Strategy* launched a second wave in the field of business strategy.

Porter focused on strategy and competition in order to take the discipline in a new direction. However, he also adopts some elements of the work of those who came before him. For example, from the scholar Kenneth Andrews* he takes the usefulness of the concept of strategy, and the important role of senior managers in identifying competitive threats and opportunities in their industry.

From the strategy scholars Paul Lawrence* and Jay Lorsch* he adopts the view that there is no single best way for a business to organize. He builds strongly on the work of the marketing analyst Sidney Schoeffler* in the Profit Impact of Marketing Strategy (PIMS)* by offering an explanation for the hole in the middle* that survey data revealed—the decisive finding that both high-revenue and low-revenue business could be profitable and that profitability was distinct from market share; businesses, Porter argues, should pursue profits.

Since the book came out, Porter's ideas have had great staying power, with business leaders adopting them in a field in which fads are commonplace. It is an indication of just how broadly they have been adopted that, for example, *Fortune* magazine, a leading business publication, called Porter "the most famous and influential business professor who has ever lived."[6]

Part of the book's strength is in stitching together industrial organization and business policy. This was a synthesis that attracted Porter—who after studying business policy at the Harvard Business School went on to study industrial organization under the economics professor Richard Caves* as a doctoral student in business economics. "There were lots of common issues but no real connection between the two fields," Porter said later in an interview.[7]

Limitations

The success of Porter's framework is limited by four factors. The first is that his analysis is focused on what might be called a "meso" level (that is, a level halfway between the macroeconomic and microeconomic), but does not take account of either. In his later books Porter extends his approach and later partly overcomes this limitation with his discussions of the value chain* and clustering* (the concentration of businesses, suppliers,* and personnel in a particular place).

A second limitation is that he does not inquire much into the nature of a company. The five forces might tell a firm that the forces of competition are relaxed enough to compete, but they do not say anything about whether the company is well suited to compete in that market.

A third limitation is that by seeking a middle ground between academic economics and business, Porter loses a certain precision in his concepts. He says, for example, "A firm differentiates itself from its competitors when it provides something unique that is valuable to buyers beyond simply offering a low price."[8] Which is differentiated here, the business or its product?

Finally, Porter's models lend a scientific justification to situations of monopoly* (only one seller of a product or service) or oligopoly* (only a few sellers). Porter's models treat these situations as perfectly normal: the result of businesses positioning themselves in their own self-interest, and with a correct interpretation of competitive forces. But while achieving a monopoly position may possibly be in the interests of the businesses concerned, it is not clear this is something the rest of society should want, especially since markets rely on competition to be efficient and keep prices down.

NOTES

1   Michael E. Porter, *Competitive Strategy: Techniques for Analyzing Industries and Competitors*, 2nd ed. (New York: Free Press, 1998), 3.

2   Nicholas Argyres and Anita McGahan, "An Interview with Michael Porter," *The Academy of Management Executive* 16:2 (May 2002): 46.

3   Argyres and McGahan, "An Interview," 46.

4   Argyres and McGahan, "An Interview," 41–42.

5   Robert E. Ankli, "Michael Porter's Competitive Advantage and Business History," *Business and Economic History* 2:21 (1992), 228–36.

6   Geoff Colvin, "There's No Quit in Michael Porter," *Fortune Magazine*, October 15, 2012, accessed February 9, 2016, http://fortune.com/2012/10/15/theres-no-quit-in-michael-porter/.

7   Argyres and McGahan, "An Interview," 43–52.

8   Porter, *Competitive Strategy*, 120.

MODULE 8
PLACE IN THE AUTHOR'S WORK

KEY POINTS

* Porter's focus throughout his life's work has been developing the ideas he first introduced in *Competitive Strategy* (1980); his book *Competitive Advantage: Creating and Sustaining Superior Performance* (1985) looks at competition* from the standpoint of an industry, and *The Competitive Advantage of Nations* (1990) looks at how countries compete with each another economically.

* His second book, *Competitive Advantage*, introduces the idea of the value chain:* the actions or processes a company carries out that can add value and increase competitive advantage.*

* In the third of these books, Porter introduces the idea of clustering*—in which countries gain advantage in particular industries by having high concentrations of related businesses, like film in Hollywood or finance in the City of London.

Positioning

Competitive Strategy: Techniques for Analyzing Industries and Competitors (1980) is Michael E. Porter's first, most widely read, and most influential work on competition, and it set him on a path of exploring different aspects of competition for the rest of his successful career as a scholar.[1] The book is based on an article that he wrote in the *Harvard Business Review* the year before, "How Competitive Forces Shape Strategy."[2] This article drew an instant audience, and received first place in the 1979 McKinsey Award given for the best *Harvard Business Review* article that year. Its principal focus is on how a business should

> 66 My initial research was in the industrial organization tradition … There came a time, though, when I decided that I was going to have to stop pursuing the trajectory I was on and take a big leap … I decided that I would seek a complete framework, drawing not only on statistical tests but on the larger number of case studies that I had by then assembled, and that was when *Competitive Strategy* was born. 99

> Nicholas Argyres and Anita McGahan, "An Interview with Michael Porter," *The Academy of Management Executive*

analyze the environment in its sector to work out what its strategy should be if it is to be successful.

Most of Porter's works after *Competitive Strategy* build on the book's ideas in some way. His body of work is vast, with 19 books and 125 articles, but it is worth highlighting two other major books that were well received.

In 1985, Porter published *Competitive Advantage: Creating and Sustaining Superior Performance* as a companion to *Competitive Strategy*.[3] This book looks at competition at the level of industries, just as *Competitive Strategy* looks at it from the point of view of a firm. If his first book was a text for ambitious young executives, his second was for chief executives—company bosses. And if part of the task of *Competitive Strategy* is determining the keys to getting ahead of the competition, *Competitive Advantage* seeks to provide wisdom about how to stay there.

Competitive Advantage introduced a key idea for which Porter is widely known: the value chain.* This is a rough model for a series of activities or processes, each of which adds value, and for which the customer is prepared to pay. Every action of a company, down to training and providing employee benefits, can be a link in the chain in its own right, and a source of advantage over competitors.

Later, in *The Competitive Advantage of Nations* (1990), Porter would expand this viewpoint to take into account how nations compete economically with one another. Among the concepts he introduces is that of a cluster of businesses in the same industry in the same place, benefiting from the sharing of knowledge. An example is a technology hub, like Silicon Valley. This allows Porter to consider how having business clusters of sufficient size is critical to a country's competitiveness.[4]

His other books tend to apply the insights in these three major works to different cases. He has looked a great deal at introducing competition into health care,[5] for example, and many of his other works have applied his principles to particular countries, such as Japan and Sweden.[6]

Integration

The five-forces analysis* and generic strategies* (from his 1980 *Competitive Strategy*) represent one part of Porter's main contribution to business; the value chain (from 1985) is another key concept for which he is known.

Porter introduces the idea of the value chain in a way that comes right to the point: "Competitive advantage cannot be understood by looking at a firm as a whole. It stems from the many discrete activities a firm performs in designing, producing, marketing, delivering and supporting its product. Each of these activities can contribute to a firm's relative cost position and create a basis for differentiation.*"[7]

This is the value chain—not a string of independent activities (although each can be measured independently). Analyzing the value chain, then, is a tool to break down a firm into a collection of strategically important processes, to understand better the effect of each on cost behavior (the way in which a product's cost changes in response to changes in a company's production activity) and differentiation.* Separate activities like design, production, marketing, and delivery, can each, by performing better than those of competitors, bring a competitive advantage.

Porter's concept of the value chain quickly joined his ideas in *Competitive Strategy* on the pages of business textbooks and in management thought. The concept has since been extended beyond individual firms, to connect value chains into a "value system"* by continuing the analysis to look at the suppliers* who supply a company's suppliers, and the buyers who buy products from a company's buyers.

Significance

Much of the significance of Porter's arguments in *Competitive Strategy* can be viewed by looking at how he explores them further in the third of his most important books, *The Competitive Advantage of Nations* (1990).

In *The Competitive Advantage of Nations*, Porter considers competitiveness, and the forces behind it, at a national level. These concerns come from his worries over dramatic and enduring declines in how competitive American business is—anxieties that he fleshes out with a good deal of evidence.

In the book, Porter also expresses further his frustrations with the limitations of neoclassical economics*—the dominant approach to economics used to study today's global economy, founded on assumptions such as the rational nature of economic decisions made in order to fulfill specific aims. One example he points to is industry clustering: the technology sector grew rapidly in San Francisco's Silicon Valley, for example, and not in a place with lower wage rates or office costs; similarly, finance has clustered in the City of London, and cinema in Hollywood. For Porter, clusters cannot be explained by mainstream economic theory; the oversimplified notions that neoclassical economics uses generate very nice models but largely useless conclusions.

Readers praised Porter's 1990 book as a wise response to simplistic criticisms that if other nations had become more competitive than the United States, they must have had help from their governments—that in some way, they cheated.[8] Instead, the text encouraged the United States to consider ways to become more competitive that were more realistic and honest, and less ideological and xenophobic* (responses, that is, that were more than reactions based on a distrust of foreigners).

Since then, his core argument—that countries compete internationally and country competitiveness can be analyzed and measured—has gained a leading place in the management literature. It has not done so, however, in the economics literature. From the viewpoint of economists, international competitiveness is a characteristic of a business, not of a nation. For Porter, this neglect of what he sees as a key issue of our day only confirms his criticism of academic economics.

NOTES

1 See Ian Jörgensen, "Michael Porter's Contribution to Strategic Management," *Revista Base (Administração e Contabilidade) de UNISINOS*, 5:3 (2008), 236–38.

2 Michael E. Porter, "How Competitive Forces Shape Strategy," *Harvard Business Review* 57.2 (1979): 137–45.

3 Michael E. Porter, *Competitive Advantage: Creating and Sustaining Superior Performance* (New York: Free Press), 1985.

4 Michael E. Porter, The *Competitive Advantage of Nations* (New York: Macmillan, 1990; 2nd ed., 1998).

5 Michael E. Porter and Elizabeth O. Teisberg, *Redefining Health Care: Creating Value-Based Competition on Results* (Boston, MA: Harvard Business School Press, 2006).

6 Michael E. Porter et al., *Can Japan Compete?* (Basingstoke, UK: Macmillan Publishing, 2000); and Michael E. Porter et al., *Advantage Sweden* (Stockholm: Norstedts Förlag, 1991).

7 Porter, *The Competitive Advantage*, 33.

8 Mariann Jelinek, "Review of *The Competitive Advantage of Nations*," *Administrative Science Quarterly* 37:3 (1992): 507–10.

SECTION 3
IMPACT

MODULE 9
THE FIRST RESPONSES

KEY POINTS

- While Porter's *Competitive Strategy* sparked great interest in management and academic literature, it has also been criticized for only providing examples to support and illustrate his ideas, even if other examples to support the counterargument could be found.

- Although Porter has answered most of his critiques in detail, he has changed his position in one area; he now believes a "hybrid" strategy, focusing on low-cost products and niche products for a slice of the market, can be profitable.

- Other readers have attempted to add a sixth force to Porter's five forces* (often the government or technology); lawyers have argued that many of the actions he suggests to make it harder for new companies to enter a market may violate antitrust* legislation (law that seeks to promote free-market competition* by preventing things such as agreements by companies on what prices they will all charge).

Criticism

The key critiques of Michael E. Porter's *Competitive Strategy: Techniques for Analyzing Industries and Competitors* are:
- Its approach to understanding rapidly changing modern business is too static.
- Porter's generic strategies* are substitutes for thought rather than spurs to original thinking.
- The underlying beliefs behind the five forces are incorrect.

> **"** Porter's books overflow with ideas which cry out to be borrowed and put to further use. **"**
>
> William Gartner, "Review of *Competitive Strategy* and *Competitive Advantage*," *The Academy of Management Review*

- His examples and his use of academic literature are selective and incomplete.
- His approach gives too much importance to the role of career managers and consultants, playing down the intuitive knowledge of lower levels of managers and experts in a business, who may have lengthier or more practical knowledge of making and selling products.

The first criticism is that Porter's model is static and a poor fit for describing a modern, rapidly changing industry.[1] A "war of position," in which producers battle to occupy low cost, high features, or niche positions in a market, like that prescribed by Porter's generic strategies, fits an age of "durable products," stable consumer needs, and well-defined markets and competitors. However, in a modern business world "the essence of strategy is not the structure of a company's product and market but the dynamics of its behavior," according to a representative group of critics. Everything is in motion, in this view, and there is no stable structure.[2]

Others have said that the five forces and three strategies are substitutes for thought, not an invitation to ponder key questions. In the words of one critic, "with the advent of generic strategies the task of the executive suddenly became much simpler. Rather than by slogging through a structured analytical process, success could be achieved by following the checklist in the latest airport [best-seller bookshop] book."[3]

The third criticism is that the intellectual beliefs underlying the five forces might be incorrect.[4] One of these assumptions is that buyers, competitors, and suppliers are unrelated, and do not coordinate their approaches, or interact. In a small industry, however, they may very well be in close and constant touch, or in larger ones they may interact at trade fairs and through industrial associations. Rather than only competing, they may see themselves as allies in supporting an industry, its well-being, and its image. Or companies may see would-be competitors as useful sources of help or expertise if their personal relationships are close, or they may outsource to each other when demand for their products is especially high.

Other beliefs that critics have questioned include the assumption that businesses have enough knowledge of the future to accurately do the type of strategic planning outlined in Porter's book. Similarly, critics have questioned the assumption that a company's economic value is augmented by barriers keeping new companies from entering a market, rather than by resources or technical skill; this "occludes [hides] the true role that employees play in the creation of innovation and value," says one group of critics.[5]

Birger Wernerfelt* of the Massachusetts Institute of Technology claims that it is not possible to evaluate an industry's attractiveness— the aim of the five forces—without looking at the resources a business brings to it. Wernerfelt developed a resource-based view* that focuses on the firm and the resources at its disposal rather than on the industry. It uses that bundle of resources as the starting point for measuring competitive advantage.*[6] Although Porter's is more broadly used, this is a major competing theory.

On the issue of the barriers that make it hard for new firms to enter a market, the business scholars Vance Fried* and Benjamin Oviatt* warn about Porter's "general disregard of US antitrust law." This collection of laws seeks to protect competition, by making it illegal for companies to engage in such activities as agreeing on the prices they will each charge. Fried and Oviatt claim that some measures Porter suggests would go against the laws. They add that "risks of violating these laws are inherent in a large number of the defensive and complementary product strategies discussed by Porter, but he generally ignores them."[7] Specifically, the authors say many actions Porter recommends to make it difficult for potential competitors to enter the market may run the risk of violating the Sherman Act,* a major piece of US antitrust legislation passed in 1890.[8]

The fourth criticism is that Porter is selective either with his examples or with his use of the academic literature. William Gartner,* a professor of business studies, suggests Porter did not choose his examples fairly, but rather to support and illustrate his ideas. According to Gartner, "A suspicion is that other examples might be found to make the counterargument and this could lead to some excellent studies."[9]

Part of this criticism, too, is that Porter has a somewhat selective view of the strategic management literature, especially research produced at places other than the Harvard Business School. According to Gartner, "Porter presents some rather weak scenario building strategies, yet he had only to look across the Charles River to see that Massachusetts Institute of Technology has been studying scenario building (system dynamics) for the last twenty years."[10] Scenario building is an approach to strategy that looks at several possible alternative futures—or scenarios—and invites a planner to consider, for example, three different futures: optimistic, pessimistic, and likely.

Finally, the Canadian academic Henry Mintzberg* has offered another approach, which stresses emergent strategy*—a strategy that emerges informally, as an alternative or supplement to senior management's official strategy. This is a response to criticisms that Porter's approach relies too heavily on top management to make all the decisions. According to one critic, "given the highly specialized character and the high-level position accorded to expert strategists," Porter's framework would prevent "any movement towards participatory management"[11] (according to which people employed at different levels in a business's structure can play a role in the business's management).

Responses

Porter answers several of these criticisms in the second edition of *Competitive Strategy*.

The first criticism, not being able to analyze and explain changes in industry, is one of the most frequent attacks against Porter's five forces. Porter addresses this argument by saying "nothing static was ever intended. Each part of the framework—industry analysis, competitor analysis, competitive positioning—stresses conditions that are subject to change."[12]

Other researchers who are sympathetic to Porter have attempted to improve his model by building time into it.[13] One example is to evaluate how consistent the five competitive forces are through past, present, and anticipated time frames, and to detect whether industry structure is fairly constant, or quickly changing.

Porter agrees with Mintzberg about the possibility of emergent strategy existing; for him, "every firm competing in an industry has a competitive strategy, whether explicit or implicit. This strategy may have been developed explicitly through a planning process or it may have evolved implicitly through the activities of the various functional departments of the firm."[14] He argues, however, that emergent (or implicit) strategy will come from each functional department of a company pursuing "approaches dictated by its professional orientation and the incentives of those in charge." For him, this is usually not as good as when top managers set an overall policy for a company. "The sum of these departmental approaches rarely equals the best strategy."[15]

Some critics have stressed that Porter's choice of academic literature and examples is selective, and point to other possible sixth forces such as government policy influencing the market, which might also affect companies' competitive positions. Porter dismisses the suggestion, saying that "there is no [invariable] relationship between the strength and influence of government and the profitability of industry. You can't say that 'government is high, industry profitability is low,' or 'government is low, industry profitability is high.'"[16]

Addressing the criticism that Porter's five forces are somehow incomplete, other sympathetic readers of *Competitive Strategy* have suggested that a sixth force should indeed be added, typically either government or technology. Some of these readers have gone so far as to extend Porter's work in this way; one leading example is the business scholars Adam Brandenburger* and Barry Naiebuff's* work extending *Competitive Strategy*'s arguments by using game theory* (mathematical models of conflict and cooperation used to study the interactions of rational decision-makers).

Brandenburger and Naiebuff look at the relationships between businesses supplying interrelated products, using the results to explain some of the dynamics behind strategic alliances between businesses.[17] They call these goods that complement rather than compete with each other "complementors."* Examples of complementors might be hot dog frankfurters and buns, or gin and tonic.

While Porter has mainly rejected these efforts, he does praise Brandenburger and Naiebuff's extension of his work to consider strategic alliances. He remains convinced that the roles of government or technology must be understood as working through the five forces.[18]

He has, however, revised his thinking about whether hybrid business strategy could exist—whether a business might successfully pursue both a low-cost strategy and a differentiation strategy (producing for a specific slice of the market) at the same time.[19] Some early evidence had suggested that companies pursuing both strategies together might have more success than companies pursuing only one of them.[20]

Conflict and Consensus

Scholars have generally agreed that Porter's text is a masterful synthesis of practical lessons from research in industrial companies over the preceding 20 years. Economists have mostly treated *Competitive Strategy* as a useful source of theories and hypotheses that later, more academic, projects could test. Business and management scholars have taken it as a starting point, with other authors suggesting ways to extend it or make changes to it. As an article in the *Harvard Business Review* put it in 2013, "Michael Porter's five forces model changed the field forever."[21]

Much of this research working to explore Porter's arguments further is presented in journals such as *Strategic Management Journal*, which was formed largely because of new interest in the subject after Porter's *Competitive Strategy*.

As a widely used business text, it certainly comes in for frequent attack. Since 2008, especially, there have been many questions concerning whether or not long-term competitive advantage in fact exists, apart from in markets sheltered from competition by government regulation.[22] Those sharply critical of how corporations were run before the financial crisis of 2008* have seized on this idea that long-term competitive advantage cannot exist as an example of a false promise made by the professional management consultant class.

Alternative approaches continue to be developed, including the resource-based view. Porter's five forces remain more widely read and used, but among a handful of authors, the resource-based view is an attractive competitor.

NOTES

1   Gregory Dess et al., *Strategic Management* (London: McGraw-Hill, 1995).

2   George Stalk et al., "Competing on Capabilities: The New Rules of Corporate Strategy," *Harvard Business Review* 70.2 (1992): 57–69.

3   Cliff Bowman, "Generic Strategies: A Substitute for Thinking?" *The Ashridge Journal* (Spring, 2008): 1.

4   Kevin Coyne and Somu Subramaniam, "Bringing Discipline to Strategy," *The McKinsey Quarterly* 4 (1996): 14–25.

5   Omar Aktouf et al., "The False Expectations of Michael Porter's Strategic Management Framework," *Problems and Perspectives in Management* 4 (2005): 181–200.

6   Birger Wernerfelt, "A Resource-Based View of the Firm," *Strategic Management Journal* 5.2 (1984): 171–80.

7   Vance Fried and Benjamin Oviatt, "Michael Porter's Missing Chapter: The Risk of Antitrust Violations," *The Academy of Management Executive* 3.1 (1989): 49–56.

8   Fried and Oviatt, "Michael Porter's Missing Chapter," 49.

9   William Gartner, "Review: *Competitive Strategy and Competitive Advantage,*" *The Academy of Management Review* 10.4 (1985): 874.

10   Gartner, "Review," 875.

11   Aktouf et al., "False Expectations," 198.

12   Michael E. Porter, *Competitive Strategy: Techniques for Analyzing Industries and Competitors*, 2nd ed. (New York: Free Press, 1998), xv.

13   Želimir Dulčić et al., "From Five Competitive Forces to Five Collaborative Forces: Revised View on Industry Structure-Firm Interrelationship," *Procedia—Social and Behavioral Sciences* 58 (2012): 1077–84.

14   Porter, *Competitive Strategy*, xxi.

15   Porter, *Competitive Strategy*, xxi.

16   Nicholas Argyres and Anita McGahan, "An Interview with Michael Porter," *The Academy of Management Executive* 16.2 (2002): 46.

17   Adam Brandenburger and Barry Nalebuff, *Co-Opetition* (New York: Crown Business, 1996).

18   Porter, *Competitive Strategy*, xv.

19   Daniel I. Prajogo, "The Relationship Between Competitive Strategies and Product Quality," *Industrial Management & Data Systems* 107.1 (2007): 69–83.

20   Peter Wright et al, "Strategic Profiles, Market Share, and Business Performance," *Industrial Management* (1990): 23–28.

21   Michael Ryall, "The New Dynamics of Competition," *Harvard Business Review* (2013): 80–87.

22   Steve Denning, "What Killed Michael Porter's Monitor Group? The One Force That Really Matters," *Forbes Magazine*, November 20, 2012, accessed January 24, 2016, http://www.forbes.com/sites/stevedenning/2012/11/20/what-killed-michael-porters-monitor-group-the-one-force-that-really-matters/#d4b96f2733c7.

MODULE 10
THE EVOLVING DEBATE

KEY POINTS

- Porter's argument has encouraged the development and widespread application of certain tools to measure his forces, like the four-firm concentration ratio* to measure market share, or the Herfindal-Hirschman index* to measure an individual firm's power in the marketplace.

- After the financial crisis of 2008,* Porter's ideas attracted a great deal of criticism—especially his view that a competitive advantage* could be maintained over time in the absence of government regulation helping one firm or another.

- Although Porter has rejected the criticisms, he does say that if he were writing his book today, he would work in newer research on the power of buyers.

Uses and Problems

The five forces* and three generic strategies*—cost leadership* (keeping the prices of products low), differentiation,* and focus—that Michael E. Porter puts forward in *Competitive Strategy: Techniques for Analyzing Industries and Competitors* have been particularly well received in the field of strategic management. Scholars there have carried out considerable experimental and theoretical analysis[1] of these ideas.

The simplicity of each has helped them be long-lived. Porter's approach was applied by auto manufacturers in the 1980s as it is by Silicon Valley start-ups (young technology companies in California) today. Porter's model led business leaders to think about competition* and profitability, instead of being distracted by less relevant things—as

> 66 Except where generated by government regulation, sustainable competitive advantage simply doesn't exist. 99
>
> Steve Denning, "What Killed Michael Porter's Monitor Group? The One Force That Really Matters." *Forbes Magazine*

was the focus with older approaches. As a writer in *The Economist* has it: "Few management ideas have been so clear or so intuitively right."[2] The clarity of Porter's approach makes it easily applied in a wide variety of contexts; it grasps the dynamics at the heart of competition.

Porter's framework encourages businesses to pose questions. This, in turn, has led to the widespread use of certain means to measure features of a business. One example is measurement of competitive rivalry, one of the five forces; there are three indexes to do this. One is the four-firm concentration ratio, which measures the market share of the four largest firms; the others are the Herfindal-Hirschman index and the Lerner index,* both of which evaluate the power of an individual firm in the marketplace. Although these three indexes came before *Competitive Strategy* they have become more popular because of the book.

The extent to which Porter's model can still be applied in today's complex business environment—given the Internet and the rapid rate of change and technological advance—has been debated widely. But at the same time, recent data-based research has nonetheless shown a strong link between the five-force analysis and a business's performance. A 2014 statistical study, for example, showed that Porter's model explained performance by the Cooperative Bank of Kenya very well.[3]

Schools of Thought

With the financial crisis of 2008,* however, Porter's ideas of sustainable competitive advantage were strongly attacked.[4] In this, he was not different from many other management experts, who also attracted criticism from the public and press for their apparent roles in the downturn.

In the political environment following the 2008 financial crisis and the resulting Occupy Movement* that protested about the harm done to society by economic inequality and by the actions of the banks, an establishment figure like Porter was an obvious target.

These criticisms were only strengthened by the 2012 bankruptcy of the Monitor Group,* a business consulting firm that Porter founded together with five Harvard colleagues in 1983, and its sale for a much diminished \$116 million. For example, the venture capitalist* Peter Gorski* wrote that "even a blindfolded chimpanzee throwing darts" at the five forces framework could select an equally good business strategy as those proposed by highly paid consultants like Porter[5] ("venture capitalist" here refers to someone who provides initial investment to enable businesses to launch, in the hope of profiting from their eventual success).

In one version of this critique, *Competitive Strategy* was flawed in its aim and the actions it proposed. According to this criticism, its aim was to discover opportunities for long-term excess profits: comfortable low-competition situations, protected by barriers keeping out competitors. Porter held up these opportunities as an easier route for profit-hungry companies. But many economists were concerned that the high profits they might produce imposed unfair costs on the consuming public. According to critics such as the former management consultant Matthew Stewart,* seeking out areas of low competition instead of going to the trouble of designing better products and services, and offering customers and society more value over the long term, presented a lazy route to success.[6]

For these critics, Porter's approach was also flawed because—they argued—long-term competitive advantage does not exist, apart from when it is generated by government regulation (for example, when government grants a monopoly position to a telephone service provider or airline). Also, sustainable above-average profits could not be predicted from the structure of the business sector. Porter's ideas could help to explain success in the past, but were "almost useless in predicting them" in the future, argued Stewart in *The Management Myth: Debunking Modern Business Philosophy* (2009).[7] But not everyone accepted this critique, with the *Wall Street Journal* describing it as "clever but unfair." The newspaper argued that Porter's contributions to understanding businesses' competitive environments are in fact considerably richer than Stewart suggests.[8]

The fact that more than 30 years after its publication Porter is still critiqued for his book *Competitive Strategy* says a great deal about its importance in the business and management world.

In Current Scholarship

Some examples of the broad uses to which *Competitive Strategy* has recently been put include scholarly work in 2015 on the competitive strategies of kindergartens[9] and the Japanese beer market.[10]

Porter has indicated that if he were to rewrite *Competitive Strategy* today, he would adapt the five forces model to build ideas from recent research into his idea of buyer bargaining power.[11] In particular, he says, he would incorporate demand-side economies of scale, such as network* or bandwagon* effects. Network effects describe the effect one user of a good or service has on its value to others—its value depends on the number of other people using it. Telephones are an example (a telephone user has more people to call), as are social networks (with more people to interact with and share pictures with). Bandwagon effects are not very different—the rate of uptake of a product increases the more it is adopted by others. For example, people see their friends using a new technology—perhaps an iPhone at the time of its first appearance in 2007—and they begin thinking about whether to buy one. People's demand for a commodity increases as the number of people using it increases.

NOTES

1   Peter Wright, "A Refinement of Porter's Strategies," *Strategic Management Journal* 8:1 (January-February 1987), 93–101.

2   *The Economist* editors, "Competitive Advantage," August 4, 2008, accessed February 9, 2016, http://www.economist.com/node/11869910.

3   Christopher Indiatsy et al., "The Application of Porter's Five Forces Model on Organization Performance: A Case of Cooperative Bank of Kenya Ltd," *European Journal of Business and Management* 6.16 (2014): 75–85.

4   Steve Denning, "What Killed Michael Porter's Monitor Group? The One Force That Really Matters," *Forbes Magazine*, November 20, 2012, accessed January 24, 2016.

5   Denning, "What Killed Michael Porter's Monitor Group?".

6   Matthew Stewart, *The Management Myth: Debunking Modern Business Philosophy* (New York: W. W. Norton, 2009), 191.

7   Stewart, *The Management Myth*, 194.

8   Philip Delves Broughton, "Bogus Theories, Bad for Business," *Wall Street Journal*, August 5, 2009, accessed January 24, 2016, http://www.wsj.com/articles/SB10001424052970204313604574329183846704634.

9   Yi-Gean Chen, "The Relationship Between Competitive Strategies of Kindergartens with Different Characteristics and Parent Satisfaction," *Journal of Global Business Management* 11.2 (2015): 76–87.

10 Kan Yamamoto, "Kirin: Business Strategies for the Japanese Beer Market," MIT MBA Thesis at the Sloan School of Management, 2015.

11 Nicholas Argyres and Anita McGahan, "Introduction: Michael Porter's 'Competitive Strategy,'" *The Academy of Management Executive* 16.2 (2002): 41–42.

MODULE 11
IMPACT AND INFLUENCE TODAY

KEY POINTS

- *Competitive Strategy* remains a key text, and one of the most widely cited, for anyone interested in business strategy and competition.*

- Other scholars have come to conclusions similar to those of Porter; that the book has been criticized so much is perhaps due to its popularity.

- For academics, Porter did not provide a single empirically tested idea, offering instead a framework and rich theories for researchers to test afterward; his book has inspired a great deal of further research.

Position

Michael E. Porter's *Competitive Strategy: Techniques for Analyzing Industries and Competitors* has had an immense influence on the business world, particularly in the field of business strategy.* He has so far written 19 books, and more than 125 academic journal articles.[1] He has taught generations of leading executives and consultants at the Harvard Business School, and his ideas on strategy are a vital part of business education worldwide.[2] The Institute on Strategy and Competitiveness, which he heads at Harvard, is dedicated to exploring the ways his research can be applied to the business world.

But it is *Competitive Strategy* for which he is best known. It contains the core of his thought, which he has spent the rest of his career refining and further exploring. *Competitive Strategy* has run to 63 printings, in 19 languages. His second book, *Competitive Advantage: Creating and Sustaining Superior Performance* (1985), has been reprinted at least 38 times.

❝ I'll never forget a senior professor telling me that my note on five-forces analysis was 'a good experiment that failed.' ❞

Nicholas Argyres and Anita McGahan, "An Interview with Michael Porter," *The Academy of Management Executive*

Competitive Strategy is also a rich source of ideas and theories for exploring how businesses respond to competitive stresses in their environment—situations that make it harder for them to compete. Porter has not only influenced business through his own writing but also indirectly, through the work of other scholars inspired by the ideas he has suggested. According to Google Scholar, an online tool that lists how many times an academic work has been cited, *Competitive Strategy* has been cited nearly 65,000 times.[3]

Interaction

Perhaps because the five-force model* is now one of the best known and most broadly used business strategy tools today, critiques have only grown more widespread.

One frequent criticism is that Porter had little good reason for choosing the particular five forces that he did.[4] Another criticism has to do with how well Porter's framework suits modern business environments, which are increasingly complex, changeable, and uncertain. The model seems unable to look ahead in any meaningful way and see how entry barriers, supply chain relationships, or new market entrants all might change—often quickly and without warning.

There have been interesting comments, too, on slightly more theoretical grounds. The Canadian business strategy scholar Henry Mintzberg* makes the case, for example, that low cost is not theoretically different from other types of differentiation, and should just be considered one possible type of differentiation. The type and scope of differentiation, says Mintzberg, should be the two dimensions on which to trace a strategy.[5]

The Continuing Debate

It is worth mentioning, too, the large amount of work based on real-world data that has taken Porter's *Competitive Strategy* as a starting point.

Research that largely confirms Porter's theories can be found in the Korean scholars Linsu Kim* and Yooncheol Lim's* 1998 article "Environment, Generic Strategies, and Performance in a Rapidly Developing Country: A Taxonomic Approach," which looks at companies in South Korea. The authors find *Competitive Strategy*'s generic strategies are more supported by the data than the models of other scholars.[6]

The business scholars Alexander Miller* and Gregory Dess's* 1993 article "Assessing Porter's (1980) Model in terms of its Generalizability, Accuracy, and Simplicity" in the *Journal of Management Studies* is typical here, too.[7] It looked at Porter's generic strategies against the outcomes of the Profit Impact of Marketing Strategy (PIMS),* a two-decade-long study that identified variables that accounted for market success. Miller and Dess found that Porter's model, while simple, captured most of the complexity of the issues.

As a broad framework, Porter's view of strategy mainly competes with the resource-based view* of the business as a "bundle of unique resources."[8] Both have their uses. Porter's five forces use an analysis that looks outward, to the surrounding market environment. The resource-based view directs the analysis inward, to what is special about the business and its human, technological, and natural resources. There have also been attempts to create a model that combines the two approaches.[9]

Recently, some have attempted to push Porter's framework further. One fairly typical effort was the "Delta model,"* created at the Massachusetts Institute of Technology (MIT) by the management and strategy scholars Arnoldo Hax* and Dean Wilde.* This was an attempt to look into lasting profitability by focusing on the bond between company and customer. It replaced competition (or even the product itself) as the main issue and instead looked at customers as being in long-term relationships with a company based on transparency and fairness. Research in this direction has focused on developing strategic options that encourage customer bonding—"locking in" customers to the business, and locking them out from competitors.[10] One example is loyalty cards; another could be better computer tools to keep track of frequent customers.

NOTES

1 Michael Porter, "Curriculum Vitae," accessed February 8, 2016, www.kozminski.edu.pl/uploads/import/kozminski/pl/default_opisy_2/3269/1/1/m._porter_-_kandydat_do_tytulu_doktora_honoris__causa_alk.doc.

2 Geoff Colvin, "There's No Quit in Michael Porter," *Fortune Magazine*, October 15, 2012, accessed January 23, 2016, http://fortune.com/2012/10/15/theres-no-quit-in-michael-porter/ .

3 Google Scholar, "Porter Competitive Strategy," accessed on January 23, 2016, https://scholar.google.com/scholar?q=Porter+Competitive+Strategy&btnG=&hl=en&as_sdt=0%2C9.

4 John O'Shaughnessy, *Competitive Marketing: A Strategic Approach* (Boston, MA: Allen & Unwin, 1984); and Richard J. Speed, "Oh Mr Porter! A Re-Appraisal of Competitive Strategy," *Marketing Intelligence and Planning*, 7:5/6 (1989): 8–11.

5 Henry Mintzberg, "Generic Strategies: Toward a Comprehensive Framework," in *Advances in Strategic Management* vol. 5, ed. Robert Lamb and Paul Shrivastava (Greenwich, CT: JAI Press, 1988), 1–67.

6 Linsu Kim and Yooncheol Lim, "Environment, Generic Strategies, and Performance in a Rapidly Developing Country: A Taxonomic Approach," *The Academy of Management Journal* 31.4 (1998): 802–27.

7   Alexander Miller and Gregory Dess, "Assessing Porter's (1980) Model in Terms of its Generalizability, Accuracy, and Simplicity," *Journal of Management Studies* 30 (1993): 553–85.

8   Suzanne Rivard et al., "Resource-Based View and Competitive Strategy: An Integrated Model of the Contribution of Information Technology to Firm Performance," *The Journal of Strategic Information Systems* 15:1 (2006): 29–50.

9   Yiannis Spanos and Spyros Lioukas, "An Examination into the Causal Logic of Rent Generation: Contrasting Porter's Strategy Framework and the Resource-Based Perspective," *Strategic Management Journal* 22.10 (2001): 907–93.

10 Arnoldo Hax, *The Delta Model: Reinventing Your Business Strategy* (New York: Springer, 2009).

MODULE 12
WHERE NEXT?

KEY POINTS

- The Internet, globalization* (increasing economic, social, and political ties across continental borders) and deregulation* (a move away from government interference in the workings of the market) each have the effect of intensifying competition.* Porter's critics and defenders disagree whether this makes his framework outdated or more relevant.

- Part of the reason Porter's contributions have survived since *Competitive Strategy* first appeared in 1980 is that his forces map neatly on to core areas of microeconomics* (economic action at the level of the individual and community) that do not date easily.

- Porter's ideas are highly influential and extremely widespread. Understanding them correctly—including their limitations and the arguments made by critics against his approach—as well as recognizing when his concepts are being incorrectly applied is crucial in management today.

Future Directions

Michael E. Porter's *Competitive Strategy: Techniques for Analyzing Industries and Competitors* is helpful for understanding business competition in the fast-changing world and into the near future. His models offer clear ways of thinking through the future effects of today's trends—such as the online world, globalization, and deregulation (ending government regulations that limit things such as which companies can compete in a market).

> **"** The way to transform health care is to realign competition with value for patients. Value in health care is the health outcome per dollar of cost expended. If all system participants have to compete on value, value will improve dramatically. **"**
>
> Michael E. Porter, *Redefining Health Care: Creating Value-Based Competition on Results*

Today's companies have access to far more information about their customers, suppliers, and competitors than was available in past years—not least through the Internet.

On the one hand, this might make it easier for a business to research information to make it more competitive, and, for example, to use the five-force analysis.* On the other, it might complicate a company's efforts by intensifying the force of competition—making it easier for customers to find substitute products, lowering the costs to consumers of switching from one company to another, and making prices transparent.

But at the same time, the Internet can help businesses tremendously, by enabling them to set up better and better systems for automated order processing and customer-relationship management and assisting them to differentiate themselves from the competition. And if they are pursuing a niche strategy, the Internet can help companies focus more closely on the desires of a target market.

It may also be worth considering two other important current trends: globalization and deregulation. Globalization extends markets beyond national borders—increasing competition based on price, and eroding the strategy of focusing on a local geographical market (witness the death of the independent corner store). For its part, deregulation—removing government regulation with the aim of increasing competition—makes it easier for new companies to enter a market where regulations may previously have limited competition.

Critics have suggested that the Internet, globalization, and deregulation invalidate Porter's models, or at least require they be drastically revised. In the introduction to the second edition of *Competitive Strategy* Porter replies that these three factors can be understood through his five forces, even without updating the model.[1]

Potential

One explanation for the durability of *Competitive Strategy*'s five forces is the neatness with which they each map into important areas of microeconomics.

"Supplier's bargaining power" relates to supply and demand theory,* cost and production theory,* and price elasticity,* all of which relate to the relationship between prices and market forces; "customers' bargaining power" relates to the exact same forces as they are influenced by and as they influence customer behavior.*

"Competitive rivalry between current players" relates to market structures,* the number of players or economic actors in the market, the size of the market, and growth rates* (the increase in the market value of the goods and services produced by an economy over time). The threat of substitutes relates to substitution effects* (according to which customers will buy cheaper goods when prices go up); the threat of new entrants to the market relates to market entry barriers*— obstacles to entering a market, such as regulations or patents.

Critics such as the business author Larry Downes,* author of an article titled "Beyond Porter,"[2] take the view that forces like information technology (computers and the Internet), globalization, and deregulation require very different analytic and business tools than those developed at the beginning of the 1980s. Yet defenders of Porter might respond that exaggerating the differences between today's digital economy and what came before is what led to earlier mistakes, like the excesses of the dot-com bubble* that occurred when exaggerated expectations for the earnings of Internet-based companies led investors to drive up their stock prices to very high levels, only to have those prices, and even some whole companies, collapse in the late 1990s.

Another response to Larry Downes's critique is that his argument can be turned against him. He argues that Porter's models are tied too much to the economic conditions of 1980. But the forces he points to as the most important ones today might soon themselves be displaced by other developments—new technologies such as wearable technology and 3D printers, or new forms of regulation coming out of concern for the environment. The bottom-line question, for evaluating Porter's models, is whether they are based in the economic conditions of their time of writing, or whether they capture longer-lasting economic realities that could be applied even in the next digital boom.

Summary

Among books on business and management, *Competitive Strategy* is in a position all its own. All of the top 20 Master of Business Administration (MBA) programs ranked by the *Financial Times* teach Porter's models as part of their strategic management courses.[3] The chief alternative approach is the resource-based theory.* But it is worth noting that Porter's *Competitive Strategy* gathers 2.6 million more hits on Google than its main resource-based view rival, Birger Wernerfelt's* article "A Resource-Based View of the Firm."[4]

Competitive Strategy argues that a business is profitable either by being cheaper, or by being different. There are no alternatives.

Porter's five competitive forces provide an easily usable framework for any business to look at its environment. His three generic strategies likewise offer clear guidance about options from which a company can select in deciding how to compete with rivals in its market.

While critics have raised important points such as the importance of not simply applying a cookie-cutter approach to strategy, Porter's ideas remain the leading wisdom in business strategic management 25 years after the publication of *Competitive Strategy*.

It is important to understand and be able to apply the powerful tools and ideas Michael E. Porter outlines in *Competitive Strategy*. But it is equally important to understand their limitations and the criticisms leveled against them and to be able to recognize when they are being used incorrectly—especially for new students of strategy.

NOTES

1   Michael E. Porter, *Competitive Strategy: Techniques for Analyzing Industries and Competitors*, 2nd ed. (New York: Free Press, 1998), xv.

2   Larry Downes, "Beyond Porter," *Context Magazine*, December 1997.

3   Amir Sasson, "Confining the Five Forces," *BI Strategy Magazine*, November 19, 2013, accessed January 24, 2016, http://www.bi.edu/bizreview/articles/confining-the-five-forces-/.

4   Birger Wernerfelt, "A Resource-Based View of the Firm," *Strategic Management Journal* 5.2 (1984): 171–80.

GLOSSARY

GLOSSARY OF TERMS

Antitrust law: law that seeks to promote free-market competition by stopping anti-competitive conduct such as agreements by companies on what prices they will all charge. Notable antitrust laws are the 1890 Sherman Act of the United States, supplemented by the Clayton Act in 1914, and the European Coal and Steel Community agreement of 1951.

Bandwagon effect: a pattern in which a product grows more popular as more people buy it; the probability an individual will purchase the product increases according to the number of other consumers who have already purchased it.

Boston Consulting Group: a leading management consulting firm, founded in 1963 in Boston. In 1968 it created the growth-share matrix; its founder, Bruce Henderson, was a great proponent of the experience curve and its implications for strategy.

Cluster Mapping Project: an effort led by Porter at the Harvard Business School, which began in 2014 and seeks to gather data on the presence of clusters in regional economies within the United States. Mapping clusters—regional concentrations of related businesses—is meant to assist regions and businesses in better understanding their competitive position.

Clusters: a concentration of businesses, suppliers, and personnel in a particular place. Michael Porter popularized the term in his 1990 book *The Competitive Advantage of Nations*. Silicon Valley is an example in technology, as is the City of London in finance or the French winemaking areas of Burgundy or Bordeaux in wine.

Comparative advantage: a theory first developed by the British economist David Ricardo in 1817, according to which nations and other agents will specialize in producing the good in which they are most efficient (the good they can make at the lowest marginal cost), and engage in international trade to purchase all other goods.

Competition: a rivalry among sellers to increase their profits, market share, and volume of sales. Classical economists such as the British economist Adam Smith in his 1776 *The Wealth of Nations* described competition as providing an incentive for firms to innovate and become more efficient.

Competitive advantage: qualities that permit an organization to outperform competitors. These may permit it (Michael Porter claims) to offer a lower cost than its rivals, or to provide a differentiated product that its competitors are not supplying, but for which there is a market.

Competitive strategy: the means available to business owners seeking to increase the profitability of their business over others.

Complementors: in many extensions of Porter's five forces model, these are businesses that sell products or services that complement those sold by another business—makers of printers and paper, for example, or distillers of gin and bottlers of tonic. The concept was first introduced by the business scholar Adam Brandenburger.

Conglomerate strategy: a business adding new goods or services to diversify into a different market unrelated to its current business.

Contingency theory: the approach that there is not one best method of leadership, but that ideal leadership differs based on the task and environment. The approach could be contrasted with Weber's work on bureaucracy or Taylor's on scientific management, both of which presented a single ideal form of management.

Corporate social responsibility: a concept that first became popular in the 1960s, holding that corporations have an obligation both to contribute to the communities and environments in which they operate and to create value for shareholders. This might include support for charity, buying fairly traded materials, and contributing to waste and pollution reduction.

Cost and production theory: relates to the creation of economic well-being through a production process, using resources to create a suitable good or service, with a particular form, quantity, and distribution.

Cost leadership: the pursuit of a competitive advantage by having the lowest operating costs in the industry, through a combination of efficiency, scale, experience, technology, and standardized products; being able therefore to offer customers the lowest price.

Customer behavior: the study of buyers and their decision-making processes, including how friends and other reference groups influence them. It breaks down the buying process into recognition of a problem, searching for information, a choice to purchase a product, and its actual purchase.

Declining industries: industries that experience negative growth or are stagnant because of declining demand for their products—industries in which unit sales are in absolute decline over a sustained period.

Delta model: an approach to strategic management based on a business's relationship with its customers, rather than on competition—as in the case of Porter's five forces. Its key points include locking in customers as a source of sustainable profitability. It was developed by the management and strategy scholars Dean Wilde and Arnoldo Hax.

Deregulation: the reduction of government rules, restrictions, or oversight in any sectors of the economy. Deregulation was a heavy feature of the economic programs of President Reagan in the United States and Prime Minister Thatcher in the United Kingdom.

Differentiation: making a product different from similar products. The idea is proposed in 1933 by Edward Chamberlin in his *Theory of Monopolistic Competition*. It is also one of Michael Porter's generic strategies.

Dot-com bubble: a speculative bubble that began in 1997 and peaked in March 2000, which saw stock market values increase quickly from growth in the Internet sector. The bubble collapsed from 1999 to 2001, with some companies, such as pets.com, failing completely, and others, such as eBay and Amazon, experiencing drastic losses in value, before going on to surpass their bubble-era peaks.

Economic geography: the study of the location of economic activities. It includes such research as spatial modeling to explain how industrial clusters emerge. The role of knowledge, transport costs, and positive externalities are all-important concepts in most research, explaining why industries sometimes develop faster in some areas than others.

Economies of scale: setup under which cost advantages that come to businesses with increasing output, as fixed costs (like the costs of machinery or buildings), are spread over more units of output, making per-unit costs decrease as scale grows.

Emergent strategy: the view that strategy develops naturally over time as a company gains knowledge about which sets of behaviors work in practice.

Experience curve: an observation that the more a task has been performed, the less time is required to perform it again. From 1968 on, Bruce Henderson and the Boston Consulting Group promoted its implications for strategy.

Financial Crisis of 2008: a severe global economic downturn that saw a worldwide drop in stock markets, many banks needing to be rescued by governments, and unemployment and drops in housing markets in many parts of the world. It was the beginning of a global decline that lasted until 2012.

Five forces and **five-force analysis:** a framework proposed by Michael Porter to understand market competition better. The forces include the threat of new entrants and substitute products, the number of rival businesses, and the bargaining powers of buyers and suppliers. According to the approach, it is easier to turn a profit in less fiercely competitive industries.

Fortune 500: an annual list compiled by *Fortune* magazine featuring 500 of the largest US corporations in terms of revenue. It was first published in 1955.

Four-firm concentration ratio: a measure of how much an industry is controlled by a small number of firms—that is, how much a given industry is an oligopoly. It measures the total market share of the four largest firms in the industry.

Game theory: mathematical models of conflict and cooperation used to understand the behavior of rational decision-makers. It was developed in the 1940s by mathematicians, and now is being used as a leading research method in economics and across the social sciences.

General Electric: an American multinational company, founded in 1892 by the inventor Thomas Edison, that normally features among the 10 largest US firms by revenue on the Fortune 500 list. Half its revenue is derived from financial services; it also has substantial presences in the energy and consumer appliance sectors.

Generic strategies: three options for businesses, proposed by Porter, concerned with the pursuit of competitive advantage in their chosen market. Businesses can either choose to compete on the grounds of lowest cost, they can differentiate themselves from other products, or they can focus on a target niche market segment.

Globalization: the process of integration of nations, accelerated by advances in transportation and communications. Ideas, technologies, and goods are all increasingly exchanged. It began on a large scale with the Industrial Revolution in the nineteenth century, and has been accelerating since then.

Great Depression: a decrease in living standards and employment, which began in 1929 in the United States, spread around the world, and lasted until the late 1930s. Worldwide gross domestic product

(GDP) fell by 15 per cent from 1929 to 1932. Unemployment in the United States rose to 25 per cent.

Growth rates: the increase in the market value, adjusted for inflation, of the goods and services produced by an economy over time. Normally the rates are measured as the percentage increase of real gross domestic product, or GDP.

Growth-share matrix: a chart created by Bruce Henderson's Boston Consulting Group in 1970 to assist businesses analyzing their product lines. It plots a business's units or products by their market shares and growth rates, dividing them as cash cows, dogs, question marks, and stars.

Herfindal–Hirschman index: a measure of a business's market share within an industry, and the amount of competition within the sector.

Hole in the middle problem: a criticism raised by Porter of the idea that companies always should seek higher market share. He found that both low-revenue and high-revenue firms could be highly profitable, and it is profitability rather than market share that a company should seek. Firms in the middle were the least profitable.

Industrial organization economics: a field of study within economics that looks at the structure of firms and markets considering complications that prevent perfect competition, such as transaction costs, limited information, and barriers to entry of new firms.

Industry structure: the number of companies competing for the same business, the numbers of customers and suppliers, new entrants, and the threat of substitute products. The insight behind the concept of industry structure is that a firm's profitability depends on the market environment in which it is operating, and not only its own behavior.

Lerner index: a measure of a firm's market power, devised in 1934 by the Russian-born British economist Abba Lerner. It reflects the ability of a firm to raise the market price of a good or service over marginal cost.

Macroeconomics: the branch of economics dealing with national, regional, and global economies, and indicators including gross domestic product, unemployment rates, and inflation.

Managerial revolution: a concept associated with the work of the management scholar James Burnham, author of *The Managerial Revolution* (1941). Burnham argued that managers had become a new modern ruling class, and that unrestricted capitalism was being replaced by a more planned and centralized society and economy.

Marginal cost: the extra cost of producing one more unit. Firms decide how much of a good to produce based on comparing the marginal cost with the sale price. If it is less than the sale price, the company will continue to produce until the two are equal.

Market entry barriers: obstacles that make it difficult for a business to enter a market. These might be regulations, intellectual property such as patents, licensing and education requirements, and economies of scale enjoyed by the leading businesses already in the sector.

Market entry: the process of a business entering a new market. It might do this by setting up an entity in the new market, by exporting directly, using a reseller or distributor, or producing products in the target market.

Market segmentation: a marketing strategy that involves dividing a large market into smaller groups of customers with common needs.

Market share: in units or revenue, the percentage of a market accounted for by a particular business. Market share is an indicator of market competitiveness—how well a business is doing against its competitors.

Market size: the number of people (or companies) in a market who are potential buyers or sellers of a product or service.

Market structure: a measure of the number of firms producing a product. In a monopoly, there is one; in an oligopoly, there are several.

Marketing myopia: a term used to describe the mistake made by businesses that focus mainly on selling products rather than on meeting the needs of customers. It is the title of a 1960 article by Theodore Levitt published in the *Harvard Business Review*.

Mass production: the production of large numbers of standardized goods, especially if done with the use of an assembly line. It became widespread with the Industrial Revolution in the late nineteenth century, and especially after Henry Ford pioneered the mass production of the Model T Ford car in 1908.

Microeconomics: a branch of economics that looks at individuals and firms and their decision-making.

Monitor Group: a business strategy consulting group founded by Michael Porter and five colleagues associated with the Harvard Business School in 1983. The firm was heavily hit by the 2008 economic crisis, and filed for bankruptcy at the end of 2012. Deloitte acquired it in January 2013.

Monopoly: a market in which one supplier (in many cases a company) controls the supply of a good or service that does not have a close substitute, and can set its price considerably above the marginal cost of production.

Monopsony: a market in which one buyer confronts multiple sellers of a product. The buyer therefore has a great deal of power to set the price.

Neoclassical economics: a set of twentieth-century approaches to economics that focuses on concepts such as marginal returns, maximized utility, equilibrium, and others. Neoclassical economics is the dominant form of economics used to study today's global economy.

Network effect: the effect one user of a good or service has on its value to other people. An example is having a telephone or being on a social network—it is more useful for me to buy a telephone or be on a social networking site if you do likewise.

Occupy Movement: a series of linked protests staged in many cities around the world against what were seen as injustices in the global financial system. It began in New York in September 2011 as the Occupy Wall Street Movement.

Oligopoly: a market in which there is a small number of businesses selling a product. With a small number of businesses in a market, they may collude to keep prices up or reduce risks; or, alternatively, they may compete more fiercely.

Opportunity cost: the value of the best alternative action to one that is taken—waiting, for example, for a customer service representative costs money corresponding to the amount of time you are waiting, and the wage rate of your time. That opportunity cost represents the money you might have earned had you not been so engaged.

Organization of Petroleum Exporting Countries (OPEC): intergovernmental organization with 13 members consisting of nations that export petroleum, including Iran, Iraq, Kuwait, Libya, the United Arab Emirates, and Saudi Arabia. OPEC was established in September 1960.

PEST analysis: a framework for noting political, economic, social, and technological factors in a business's environment. It sometimes is expanded to SLEPT if including legal factors, or changed to PESTLE to include legal and environmental factors.

Porter hypothesis: a suggestion, made by Michael Porter in an article in 1995, that stricter environmental regulation might bring about efficiency and innovation in a market, which would in turn make a market more competitive.

Position/positioning: the niche that a brand occupies relative to its competitors. It is largely achieved through advertising—marking the product or service as budget or premium, entry-level or high-end, or promoting the distinctive features of the brand, such as what it can do that competitors' products cannot.

Price elasticity: a measure of how much the demand for a good or service changes in response to a change in its price.

Production orientation: when a company focuses on the good or service it produces; normally this is contrasted with a (superior) market orientation, which involves a focus on the desires of the customer.

Profit Impact of Marketing Strategy (PIMS): a survey, begun in the 1960s by Sidney Schoeffler and lasting until 1983, which researched 2,600 business units within 200 companies, and identified 37 variables that accounted for most business success. These included a strong market position, a high quality product, lower costs, and market growth.

Resource-based view: a way of conceiving of a business's competitive advantage by looking primarily at the resources—tangible or intangible—at the disposal of the business. To enjoy a lasting competitive advantage, a business's resources must be valuable, rare, hard to copy, and nonsubstitutable.

Ryanair: an Irish low-cost airline founded in 1984 and presently managed by chief executive Michael O'Leary. It is the busiest airline internationally by the number of passengers. It pioneered a low-cost business model in the context of deregulation of European aviation in 1997 and pioneered online ticket booking and no-frills, low-cost travel.

Sherman Act: an 1890 antitrust law permitting the US federal government to go after trusts and monopolies in order to promote competition in the economy.

Stanford Research International: a research institute founded in 1946 by Stanford University in California to support economic development in the surrounding region.

Strategic fit: a measure of how well the structure and capabilities of a firm matches its external environment. It is related to the resource-based view, which links profitability and lasting competitive advantage with a company's resources and capabilities.

Strategic positioning: a company's decisions about how it will create value differently from its rivals; typically, these involve a decision about whether to charge a premium price or seek lower costs for the company.

Strategy: a plan to achieve goals in a situation of uncertainty. Strategy emerged as a topic in business and management in the 1960s; previously it was associated chiefly with diplomatic or military and naval matters.

Structure–conduct–performance paradigm: a model in industrial organization economics, developed by the economist Joe Bain, which looks at how market structure affects a business's performance.

Substitutes: alternative, cheaper products or services.

Substitution effects: the effects caused by changes in the price of an item—when the price goes up, customers will buy more lower-priced goods and fewer more expensive ones. They will substitute less expensive goods for ones whose price has increased.

Suppliers: companies that supply resources a business requires to function—a wheat farm for a flour maker, a flour mill for a baker.

Supply and demand theory: an economic model of determining price in a market under conditions of competition. In a market, the price for a good will settle at the point at which the quantity supplied will match the quantity demanded.

Sustainable competitive advantage: a long-term advantage that cannot easily be duplicated or improved upon by rivals. This may consist of superior access to natural or human resources or barriers to entry in the market that shield a company from competition.

Switching costs: costs that a customer or business incurs when it changes suppliers, products, or brands.

SWOT analysis: a technique to analyze a business's Strengths, Weaknesses, Opportunities, and Threats. It was popularized by the Stanford Research Institute and Albert Humphrey in the 1960s and 1970s.

Value chain: a set of discrete activities a business performs to produce a product or service. The idea is to think of a firm's activities as a series of processes—the outputs of some processes being inputs into later ones. Michael Porter proposes the concept in his 1985 work *Competitive Advantage*.

Value system: The idea of a value system extends the concept of a value chain beyond individual firms—linking processes between the companies that produce a company's supplies and buy a company's products.

Venture capitalist: an investor who specializes in providing capital to companies in their early stages.

Vertical integration: a setup in which each element in the supply chain for a good or service is owned by a single company. The US industrialist Andrew Carnegie provided an early example in his steel manufacture.

World War II: a global war that lasted from 1939 to 1945, directly involving more than 100 million people from 30 countries and with 50–85 million deaths. Its results included decolonization in Asia and Africa, the Cold War between rival blocs led by the United States and the Soviet Union, and political integration within Europe.

Wright-Patterson Air Force Base: one of the US Air Force's largest bases, situated near Dayton, Ohio. Test flights of newly developed aircraft are frequently carried out there.

Xenophobia: an aggressive dislike or fear of people from other countries or cultures.

PEOPLE MENTIONED IN THE TEXT

Alexander the Great or **Alexander III of Macedon (365–323 B.C.E.)** was king of the Southern European nation of Macedonia from 336, of Persia (from 330), and pharaoh of Egypt (from 332). He was founder of a number of cities that bear his name, such as Alexandria in Egypt, and responsible for the widespread diffusion of Hellenic (ancient Greek) culture. His tutor was the philosopher Aristotle.

Kenneth Andrews (1916–2005) was a lecturer at the Harvard Business School and an important early figure in the spread of the concept of business strategy, together with his colleague Alfred Chandler. For Andrews, managers obtain authority by treating subordinates with respect, and organizations, to survive, require effectiveness (the ability to accomplish shared goals) and efficiency (satisfying the motives of individuals).

Joseph ("Joe") Bain (1912–91) was an economist at the University of California, Berkeley, where he was an important figure in industrial organization economics. He developed the concept of barriers to entry to explain industry performance, and worked on questions relating to industry concentration as well.

Chester Barnard (1886–1961) was a business academic known for his 1938 book *The Functions of the Executive*.

Adam Brandenburger was an academic at the Harvard Business School from 1987 to 2002, and coauthor (with Barry Nalebuff) of *Co-Opetition* (1996), which looks at situations in which companies may choose to cooperate rather than compete.

Richard Caves (b. 1931) is an economics professor at Harvard, who works especially in the area of industrial organization.

Alfred DuPont Chandler (1918–2007) was a business historian at Harvard Business School who received the Pulitzer prize for history for his 1977 book, *The Visible Hand: The Managerial Revolution in American Business.* In this book and elsewhere, he was significant in introducing and popularizing the concept of business strategy.

Gregory Dess is a management academic in Texas, known mainly for an article in the *Academy of Management Review* that looks at connections between a firm's entrepreneurial behavior and high performance.

Larry Downes is an author and business academic in the United States, known especially for his book, coauthored with Chunka Mui, *Unleashing the Killer App: Digital Strategies for Market Dominance* (2008).

Henry Ford (1863–1947) was an American industrialist and car manufacturer known especially for pioneering the assembly line and mass marketing the automobile to the middle classes.

Vance Fried is the Riata Professor of Entrepreneurship at Oklahoma State University.

William Gartner (b. 1953) is an American business studies professor at the California Lutheran University in Thousands Oaks, California, and the Copenhagen Business School in Denmark. He is an expert in entrepreneurship.

Peter Gorski is a venture capitalist and project manager in the United States, as well as an occasional author.

Arnoldo Hax is the Alfred P. Sloan Professor of Management Emeritus at the Massachusetts Institute of Technology (MIT), and specializes in strategic management. He is known for coauthoring the book *The Delta Project: Discovering New Sources of Profitability in a Networked Economy* with Dean Wilde in 2001.

Bruce Henderson (1915–92) was founder in 1963 of the Boston Consulting Group (BCG), and continued as its president and chief executive until 1980. He was very influential in the firm, deciding that its emphasis would lie in strategy consultancy. During his time at BCG, he played a major role in diffusing the concepts of the experience curve and growth-share matrix.

Albert Humphrey (1926–2005) was a management consultant and business academic who, during his time at the Stanford Research Institute, was influential in spreading the SWOT analysis.

Linsu Kim is professor of management at Korea University in South Korea.

Mark Kramer is a frequent collaborator with Michael Porter in the *Harvard Business Review*, and is especially known for his work on the concept of shared value.

Paul Lawrence (1922–2011) was the professor of organizational behavior at the Harvard Business School, known especially for his work with the organizational theorist Jay Lorsch on differentiation and integration in complex organizations.

Theodore Levitt (1925–2006) was a German-born economist at the Harvard Business School especially known for the 1960 article

"Marketing Myopia" in the *Harvard Business Review*, and for publicizing the concept of globalization.

Yooncheol Lim is an academic at the Korea Advanced Institute of Science and Technology in South Korea.

Jay Lorsch (b. 1932) is an organizational theorist at the Harvard Business School, especially known for his contributions to contingency theory—which argues that there is not a single superior style of leadership, but that leadership must take into account the environment, and aim at such goals as winning the respect of followers, providing adequately structured tasks, and having the required formal authority.

Joan Magretta is a senior associate at the Institute for Strategy and Competitiveness at the Harvard Business School, which Porter runs. Previously she has been the strategy editor of the *Harvard Business Review*, and a consultant at Bain & Company. She wrote a 2011 book on Porter, called *Understanding Michael Porter: The Essential Guide to Competition and Strategy*.

Roger Martin is dean of the University of Toronto's Rotman School of Business.

Alexander Miller is a business academic at the University of Tennessee. Among his publications is a textbook published in 1997 called *Strategic Management*.

Henry Mintzberg (b. 1939) is a Canadian academic and the Cleghorn Professor of Management Studies at McGill University, where he has taught since 1968. A specialist in business strategy, he takes a critical attitude toward received wisdom and prolific practice in management and management consultancy. He has stressed the importance of what he calls emergent strategy, arising informally within an organization—as opposed to deliberate strategy imposed by senior management, often with the assistance of consultants.

Barry Naiebuff is a researcher working on business strategy and game theory, and is the Milton Steinbach Professor of Management at the Yale School of Management. One book for which he is especially known is *Co-Opetition* (1996), coauthored with Adam Brandenburger, which looks at situations in which companies may cooperate with one another.

Benjamin Oviatt is an associate professor in the school of management at Georgia State University.

David Ricardo (1772–1823) was a British economist. He is best remembered for his work on comparative advantage, claiming that a nation should concentrate on those industries in which it is most competitive internationally. He served as a reformist member of parliament for the last four years of his life.

Philip II of Macedon (382–336 B.C.E.) was king of the ancient Greek kingdom of Macedon from 359 until his assassination, greatly expanding Macedonian territory in that time. He was father of Alexander the Great.

Sidney Schoeffler is a marketing analyst; he was one of the founders of the Profit Impact of Marketing Strategy research project, begun at General Electric in the 1960s, which looked into why some business units were more profitable than others, and evaluated them in terms of their market position and strategies.

Herbert Simon (1916–2001) was an American academic and student of decision-making who received the Nobel Prize in Economics in 1978. One of his contributions was to discuss decision-making in the context of uncertainty.

Matthew Stewart (b. 1963) is an author and philosopher living in Boston, who worked as a management consultant after completing a DPhil in philosophy at the University of Oxford in 1988. He wrote critically about his experiences as a management consultant, and about the consultancy industry, in his book *The Management Myth: Debunking the Modern Philosophy of Business*, published in 2009 by W. W. Norton.

Frederick Winslow Taylor (1856–1915) was one of the first management consultants and an American mechanical engineer. In a 1911 book, *The Principles of Scientific Management*, he sought to apply principles from engineering to making industries more efficient. He was one of the leaders of the Efficiency Movement, which also is called Taylorism.

Mark Twain (1835–1910) is the pen name of the American author Samuel Clemens, author of *The Adventures of Tom Sawyer* in 1876 and its sequel *Adventures of Huckleberry Finn* in 1885. He was the subject of a doctoral dissertation by Kenneth Andrews, subsequently a leading management scholar.

Birger Wernerfelt (b. 1951) is a Danish economist and management academic, and holds the JC Penney professorship of management at MIT. He is best known for proposing the resource-based view of the firm in a 1984 journal article.

Dean Wilde is a strategy consultant and visiting professor of strategy at the MIT Sloan School of Management, who with Arnoldo Hax coauthored the book *The Delta Project: Discovering New Sources of Profitability in a Networked Economy.*

WORKS CITED

WORKS CITED

Aktouf, Omar, Miloud Chenoufi, and David Holford. "The False Expectations of Michael Porter's Strategic Management Framework." *Problems and Perspectives in Management* 4 (2005): 181–200.

Andrews, Kenneth R. *The Concept of Corporate Strategy.* Homewood, IL: R.D. Irwin, 1994.

Ankli, Robert E. "Michael Porter's Competitive Advantage and Business History." *Business and Economic History* 21 (1992): 228–36.

Argyres, Nicholas, and Anita McGahan. "An Interview with Michael Porter." *The Academy of Management Executive* 16.2 (May 2002): 43–52.

"Introduction: Michael Porter's *Competitive Strategy.*" *The Academy of Management Executive* 16:2 (May 2002): 41–42.

Bain, Joseph S. *Industrial Organization.* New York: John Wiley & Sons, Inc., 1959.

Barnard, Chester. *The Functions of the Executive.* Cambridge, MA: Harvard University Press, 1938.

Bedeian, Arthur, and Daniel Wren. "Most Influential Management Books of the 20th Century." *Organizational Dynamics* 29:3 (Winter 2001): 221–25.

Brandenburger, Adam, and Barry Nalebuff. *Co-Opetition.* New York: Crown Business, 1996.

Bowman, Cliff. "Generic Strategies: A Substitute for Thinking?" *The Ashridge Journal* (2008): 1–28.

Broughton, Philip Delves. "Bogus Theories, Bad for Business." *Wall Street Journal*, August 5, 2009. Accessed January 24, 2016. http://www.wsj.com/articles/SB10001424052970204313604574329183846704634.

Chandler, Alfred. *The Visible Hand: The Managerial Revolution in American Business.* Cambridge, MA: Belknap Press, 1977.

Strategy and Structure: Chapters in the History of the American Industrial Enterprise. Cambridge, MA: MIT Press, 1962.

Chen, Yi-Gean. "The Relationship Between Competitive Strategies of Kindergartens with Different Characteristics and Parent Satisfaction." *Journal of Global Business Management* 11.2 (2015): 76–87.

Colvin, Geoff. "There's No Quit in Michael Porter." *Fortune Magazine*, October 15, 2012. Accessed February 9, 2016. http://fortune.com/2012/10/15/theres-no-quit-in-michael-porter/.

Coyne, Kevin, and Somu Subramaniam. "Bringing Discipline to Strategy." *The McKinsey Quarterly* 4 (1996): 14–25.

Denning, Steve. "What Killed Michael Porter's Monitor Group? The One Force That Really Matters." *Forbes Magazine*, November 20, 2012. Accessed January 24, 2016. http://www.forbes.com/sites/stevedenning/2012/11/20/what-killed-michael-porters-monitor-group-the-one-force-that-really-matters/#d4b96f2733c7.

Dess, Gregory, Tom Lumpkin, Alan Eisner, and Gerry McNamara. *Strategic Management*. London: McGraw-Hill, 1995.

Downes, Larry. "Beyond Porter." *Context Magazine* December 1997.

Dulčić, Želimir, Vladimir Gnjidić, and Nikša Alfirević. "From Five Competitive Forces to Five Collaborative Forces: Revised View on Industry Structure-Firm Interrelationship." *Procedia—Social and Behavioral Sciences* 58 (2012): 1077–84.

Economist, The, editors. "Competitive Advantage." *The Economist*, August 4, 2008. Accessed February 8, 2016. www.economist.com/node/11869910.

"The Experience Curve." *The Economist*, September 14, 2009. Accessed February 8, 2016. http://www.economist.com/node/14298944.

Ford, Henry, with Samuel Crowther. *My Life and Work*. Garden City, NY: Doubleday, Page, 1923.

Fried, Vance, and Benjamin Oviatt. "Michael Porter's Missing Chapter: The Risk of Antitrust Violations." *The Academy of Management Executive*, 3.1 (1989): 49–56.

Gartner, William. "Review: *Competitive Strategy* and *Competitive Advantage*." *The Academy of Management Review* 10.4 (1985): 873–75.

Google Scholar. "Porter Competitive Strategy." Accessed on January 23, 2016. https://scholar.google.com/scholar?q=Porter+Competitive+Strategy&btnG=&hl=en&as_sdt=0%2C9

"Porter Hypothesis." Accessed January 29, 2016. https://scholar.google.com/scholar?hl=en&q=%22Porter+Hypothesis%22&btnG=&as_sdt=1%2C9&as_sdtp=.

Hall, David, and Maurice Saias. "Strategy Follows Structure!" *Strategic Management Journal* 1.2 (1980): 149–63.

Hax, Arnoldo. *The Delta Model: Reinventing Your Business Strategy*. New York: Springer, 2009.

Indiatsy, Christopher, Muchero Mwangi, Evans Mandere, Julius Bichanga, and Gongera George. "The Application of Porter's Five Forces Model on Organization Performance: A Case of Cooperative Bank of Kenya Ltd." *European Journal of*

Business and Management 6.16 (2014): 75–85.

Institute for Strategy and Competitiveness. "Home." Accessed January 29, 2016, http://www.isc.hbs.edu/.

Jelinek, Mariann. "Review of *The Competitive Advantage of Nations.*" *Administrative Science Quarterly* 37.3 (1992): 507–10.

Jörgensen, Ian. "Michael Porter's Contribution to Strategic Management." *Revista Base (Administração e Contabilidade) de UNISINOS* 5.3 (2008): 236–38.

Kiechel, Walter. *The Lords of Strategy: The Secret Intellectual History of the New Corporate World.* Cambridge, MA: Harvard Business Press, 2010.

Kim, Linsu, and Yooncheol Lim. "Environment, Generic Strategies, and Performance in a Rapidly Developing Country: A Taxonomic Approach." *The Academy of Management Journal* 31.4 (1998): 802–27.

Lawrence, Paul, and Jay Lorsch. *Organization and Environment*. Boston, MA: Harvard Business School, Division of Research,1967.

Learned, Philip, C. Roland Christensen, Kenneth R. Andrews, and William Guth. *Business Policy: Text and Cases*. Homewood, IL: R.D. Irwin, 1969.

Levitt, Theodore. "Marketing Myopia." *Harvard Business Review* (1960): 45–56.

Magretta, Joan. *Understanding Michael Porter: The Essential Guide to Competition and Strategy*. Cambridge, MA: Harvard Business Review Press, 2011.

Miller, Alex, and Gregory Dess. "Assessing Porter's (1980) Model in Terms of its Generalizability, Accuracy, and Simplicity." *Journal of Management Studies* 30 (1993): 553–85.

Mintzberg, Henry. "Generic Strategies: Toward a Comprehensive Framework." In *Advances in Strategic Management* vol. 5, edited by Robert Lamb and Paul Shrivastava, 1–67. Greenwich, CT: JAI Press, 1988.

Nieto-Rodriguez, Antonio. *The Focused Organization: How Concentrating on a Few Key Initiatives Can Dramatically Improve Strategy Execution*. Burlington, VT: Ashgate, 2012.

O'Shaughnessy, John. *Competitive Marketing: A Strategic Approach*. Boston, MA: Allen & Unwin, 1984.

Porter, Michael. *Competitive Advantage: Creating and Sustaining Superior Performance.* New York: Free Press, 1985.

The Competitive Advantage of Nations. New York: Macmillan, 1990; 2d ed., 1998.

Competitive Strategy: Techniques for Analyzing Industries and Competitors, 2nd ed. New York: Free Press, 1998.

"Curriculum Vitae." Accessed February 8, 2016. www.kozminski.edu.pl/uploads/import/kozminski/pl/default_opisy_2/3269/1/1/m._porter_-_kandydat_do_tytulu_doktora_honoris__causa_alk.doc.

"How Competitive Forces Shape Strategy." *Harvard Business Review* 57.2 (1979): 86–93.

Porter, Michael E., and Mark R. Kramer. "Creating Shared Value." *Harvard Business Review* (2011): 63–70.

Porter, Michael E., Orjan Solvell, and I. Zander. *Advantage Sweden.* Stockholm: Norstedts Förlag, 1991.

Porter, Michael E., Hirotaka Takeuchi, and M. Sakakibara. *Can Japan Compete?* Basingstoke, UK: Macmillan Publishing, 2000.

Porter, Michael E., and Elizabeth O. Teisberg. *Redefining Health Care: Creating Value-Based Competition on Results.* Boston, MA: Harvard Business School Press, 2006.

Prajogo, Daniel I. "The Relationship Between Competitive Strategies and Product Quality." *Industrial Management & Data Systems* 107.1 (2007): 69–83.

Rivard, Suzanne, Louis Raymond, and David Verreault. "Resource-Based View and Competitive Strategy: An Integrated Model of the Contribution of Information Technology to Firm Performance." *The Journal of Strategic Information Systems* 15.1 (2006): 29–50.

Ryall, Michael. "The New Dynamics of Competition." *Harvard Business Review* (2013): 80–87.

Sasson, Amir. "Confining the Five Forces." *BI Strategy Magazine*, November 19, 2013. Accessed January 24, 2016. http://www.bi.edu/bizreview/articles/confining-the-five-forces-/.

Simon, Herbert. *Administrative Behavior: A Study of Decision-Making Processes in Administrative Organizations.* New York: Macmillan, 1947.

Slater, Stanley, and Thomas Zwirlein. "Shareholder Value and Investment Strategy Using the General Portfolio Model." *Journal of Management* 18.4 (1992): 717–32.

Spanos, Yiannis E., and Spyros Lioukas. "An Examination into the Causal Logic of Rent Generation: Contrasting Porter's Strategy Framework and the Resource-Based Perspective." *Strategic Management Journal* 22.10 (2001): 907–93.

Speed, Richard J. «Oh Mr Porter! A Re-Appraisal of Competitive Strategy.» *Marketing Intelligence and Planning* 7.5/6 (1989): 8–11.

Stalk, George, Philip Evans, and Lawrence Shulman. "Competing on Capabilities: The New Rules of Corporate Strategy." *Harvard Business Review* 70.2 (1992): 57–69.

Stewart, Matthew. *The Management Myth: Debunking Modern Business Philosophy.* New York: W. W. Norton, 2009.

Taylor, Frederick Winslow. *The Principles of Scientific Management*. New York: Harper Brothers, 1911.

Wernerfelt, Birger. "A Resource-Based View of the Firm." *Strategic Management Journal* 5.2 (1984): 171–80.

Wright, Peter. "A Refinement of Porter's Strategies." *Strategic Management Journal* 8.1 (1987): 93–101.

Wright, Peter, Mark Kroll, Ben Kedia, and Charles Pringle. "Strategic Profiles, Market Share, and Business Performance." *Industrial Management* (1990): 23–28.

Yamamoto, Kan. "Kirin: Business Strategies for the Japanese Beer Market." MIT MBA Thesis at the Sloan School of Management, 2015.

THE MACAT LIBRARY
BY DISCIPLINE

The Macat Library By Discipline

AFRICANA STUDIES

Chinua Achebe's *An Image of Africa: Racism in Conrad's Heart of Darkness*
W. E. B. Du Bois's *The Souls of Black Folk*
Zora Neale Huston's *Characteristics of Negro Expression*
Martin Luther King Jr's *Why We Can't Wait*
Toni Morrison's *Playing in the Dark: Whiteness in the American Literary Imagination*

ANTHROPOLOGY

Arjun Appadurai's *Modernity at Large: Cultural Dimensions of Globalisation*
Philippe Ariès's *Centuries of Childhood*
Franz Boas's *Race, Language and Culture*
Kim Chan & Renée Mauborgne's *Blue Ocean Strategy*
Jared Diamond's *Guns, Germs & Steel: the Fate of Human Societies*
Jared Diamond's *Collapse: How Societies Choose to Fail or Survive*
E. E. Evans-Pritchard's *Witchcraft, Oracles and Magic Among the Azande*
James Ferguson's *The Anti-Politics Machine*
Clifford Geertz's *The Interpretation of Cultures*
David Graeber's *Debt: the First 5000 Years*
Karen Ho's *Liquidated: An Ethnography of Wall Street*
Geert Hofstede's *Culture's Consequences: Comparing Values, Behaviors, Institutes and Organizations across Nations*
Claude Lévi-Strauss's *Structural Anthropology*
Jay Macleod's *Ain't No Makin' It: Aspirations and Attainment in a Low-Income Neighborhood*
Saba Mahmood's *The Politics of Piety: The Islamic Revival and the Feminist Subject*
Marcel Mauss's *The Gift*

BUSINESS

Jean Lave & Etienne Wenger's *Situated Learning*
Theodore Levitt's *Marketing Myopia*
Burton G. Malkiel's *A Random Walk Down Wall Street*
Douglas McGregor's *The Human Side of Enterprise*
Michael Porter's *Competitive Strategy: Creating and Sustaining Superior Performance*
John Kotter's *Leading Change*
C. K. Prahalad & Gary Hamel's *The Core Competence of the Corporation*

CRIMINOLOGY

Michelle Alexander's *The New Jim Crow: Mass Incarceration in the Age of Colorblindness*
Michael R. Gottfredson & Travis Hirschi's *A General Theory of Crime*
Richard Herrnstein & Charles A. Murray's *The Bell Curve: Intelligence and Class Structure in American Life*
Elizabeth Loftus's *Eyewitness Testimony*
Jay Macleod's *Ain't No Makin' It: Aspirations and Attainment in a Low-Income Neighborhood*
Philip Zimbardo's *The Lucifer Effect*

ECONOMICS

Janet Abu-Lughod's *Before European Hegemony*
Ha-Joon Chang's *Kicking Away the Ladder*
David Brion Davis's *The Problem of Slavery in the Age of Revolution*
Milton Friedman's *The Role of Monetary Policy*
Milton Friedman's *Capitalism and Freedom*
David Graeber's *Debt: the First 5000 Years*
Friedrich Hayek's *The Road to Serfdom*
Karen Ho's *Liquidated: An Ethnography of Wall Street*

John Maynard Keynes's *The General Theory of Employment, Interest and Money*
Charles P. Kindleberger's *Manias, Panics and Crashes*
Robert Lucas's *Why Doesn't Capital Flow from Rich to Poor Countries?*
Burton G. Malkiel's *A Random Walk Down Wall Street*
Thomas Robert Malthus's *An Essay on the Principle of Population*
Karl Marx's *Capital*
Thomas Piketty's *Capital in the Twenty-First Century*
Amartya Sen's *Development as Freedom*
Adam Smith's *The Wealth of Nations*
Nassim Nicholas Taleb's *The Black Swan: The Impact of the Highly Improbable*
Amos Tversky's & Daniel Kahneman's *Judgment under Uncertainty: Heuristics and Biases*
Mahbub Ul Haq's *Reflections on Human Development*
Max Weber's *The Protestant Ethic and the Spirit of Capitalism*

FEMINISM AND GENDER STUDIES

Judith Butler's *Gender Trouble*
Simone De Beauvoir's *The Second Sex*
Michel Foucault's *History of Sexuality*
Betty Friedan's *The Feminine Mystique*
Saba Mahmood's *The Politics of Piety: The Islamic Revival and the Feminist Subjec*t
Joan Wallach Scott's *Gender and the Politics of History*
Mary Wollstonecraft's *A Vindication of the Rights of Woman*
Virginia Woolf's *A Room of One's Own*

GEOGRAPHY

The Brundtland Report's *Our Common Future*
Rachel Carson's *Silent Spring*
Charles Darwin's *On the Origin of Species*
James Ferguson's *The Anti-Politics Machine*
Jane Jacobs's *The Death and Life of Great American Cities*
James Lovelock's *Gaia: A New Look at Life on Earth*
Amartya Sen's *Development as Freedom*
Mathis Wackernagel & William Rees's *Our Ecological Footprint*

HISTORY

Janet Abu-Lughod's *Before European Hegemony*
Benedict Anderson's *Imagined Communities*
Bernard Bailyn's *The Ideological Origins of the American Revolution*
Hanna Batatu's *The Old Social Classes And The Revolutionary Movements Of Iraq*
Christopher Browning's *Ordinary Men: Reserve Police Batallion 101 and the Final Solution in Poland*
Edmund Burke's *Reflections on the Revolution in France*
William Cronon's *Nature's Metropolis: Chicago And The Great West*
Alfred W. Crosby's *The Columbian Exchange*
Hamid Dabashi's *Iran: A People Interrupted*
David Brion Davis's *The Problem of Slavery in the Age of Revolution*
Nathalie Zemon Davis's *The Return of Martin Guerre*
Jared Diamond's *Guns, Germs & Steel: the Fate of Human Societies*
Frank Dikotter's *Mao's Great Famine*
John W Dower's *War Without Mercy: Race And Power In The Pacific War*
W. E. B. Du Bois's *The Souls of Black Folk*
Richard J. Evans's *In Defence of History*
Lucien Febvre's *The Problem of Unbelief in the 16th Century*
Sheila Fitzpatrick's *Everyday Stalinism*

The Macat Library By Discipline

Eric Foner's *Reconstruction: America's Unfinished Revolution, 1863-1877*
Michel Foucault's *Discipline and Punish*
Michel Foucault's *History of Sexuality*
Francis Fukuyama's *The End of History and the Last Man*
John Lewis Gaddis's *We Now Know: Rethinking Cold War History*
Ernest Gellner's *Nations and Nationalism*
Eugene Genovese's *Roll, Jordan, Roll: The World the Slaves Made*
Carlo Ginzburg's *The Night Battles*
Daniel Goldhagen's *Hitler's Willing Executioners*
Jack Goldstone's *Revolution and Rebellion in the Early Modern World*
Antonio Gramsci's *The Prison Notebooks*
Alexander Hamilton, John Jay & James Madison's *The Federalist Papers*
Christopher Hill's *The World Turned Upside Down*
Carole Hillenbrand's *The Crusades: Islamic Perspectives*
Thomas Hobbes's *Leviathan*
Eric Hobsbawm's *The Age Of Revolution*
John A. Hobson's *Imperialism: A Study*
Albert Hourani's *History of the Arab Peoples*
Samuel P. Huntington's *The Clash of Civilizations and the Remaking of World Order*
C. L. R. James's *The Black Jacobins*
Tony Judt's *Postwar: A History of Europe Since 1945*
Ernst Kantorowicz's *The King's Two Bodies: A Study in Medieval Political Theology*
Paul Kennedy's *The Rise and Fall of the Great Powers*
Ian Kershaw's *The "Hitler Myth": Image and Reality in the Third Reich*
John Maynard Keynes's *The General Theory of Employment, Interest and Money*
Charles P. Kindleberger's *Manias, Panics and Crashes*
Martin Luther King Jr's *Why We Can't Wait*
Henry Kissinger's *World Order: Reflections on the Character of Nations and the Course of History*
Thomas Kuhn's *The Structure of Scientific Revolutions*
Georges Lefebvre's *The Coming of the French Revolution*
John Locke's *Two Treatises of Government*
Niccolò Machiavelli's *The Prince*
Thomas Robert Malthus's *An Essay on the Principle of Population*
Mahmood Mamdani's *Citizen and Subject: Contemporary Africa And The Legacy Of Late Colonialism*
Karl Marx's *Capital*
Stanley Milgram's *Obedience to Authority*
John Stuart Mill's *On Liberty*
Thomas Paine's *Common Sense*
Thomas Paine's *Rights of Man*
Geoffrey Parker's *Global Crisis: War, Climate Change and Catastrophe in the Seventeenth Century*
Jonathan Riley-Smith's *The First Crusade and the Idea of Crusading*
Jean-Jacques Rousseau's *The Social Contract*
Joan Wallach Scott's *Gender and the Politics of History*
Theda Skocpol's *States and Social Revolutions*
Adam Smith's *The Wealth of Nations*
Timothy Snyder's *Bloodlands: Europe Between Hitler and Stalin*
Sun Tzu's *The Art of War*
Keith Thomas's *Religion and the Decline of Magic*
Thucydides's *The History of the Peloponnesian War*
Frederick Jackson Turner's *The Significance of the Frontier in American History*
Odd Arne Westad's *The Global Cold War: Third World Interventions And The Making Of Our Times*

LITERATURE

Chinua Achebe's *An Image of Africa: Racism in Conrad's Heart of Darkness*
Roland Barthes's *Mythologies*
Homi K. Bhabha's *The Location of Culture*
Judith Butler's *Gender Trouble*
Simone De Beauvoir's *The Second Sex*
Ferdinand De Saussure's *Course in General Linguistics*
T. S. Eliot's *The Sacred Wood: Essays on Poetry and Criticism*
Zora Neale Huston's *Characteristics of Negro Expression*
Toni Morrison's *Playing in the Dark: Whiteness in the American Literary Imagination*
Edward Said's *Orientalism*
Gayatri Chakravorty Spivak's *Can the Subaltern Speak?*
Mary Wollstonecraft's *A Vindication of the Rights of Women*
Virginia Woolf's *A Room of One's Own*

PHILOSOPHY

Elizabeth Anscombe's *Modern Moral Philosophy*
Hannah Arendt's *The Human Condition*
Aristotle's *Metaphysics*
Aristotle's *Nicomachean Ethics*
Edmund Gettier's *Is Justified True Belief Knowledge?*
Georg Wilhelm Friedrich Hegel's *Phenomenology of Spirit*
David Hume's *Dialogues Concerning Natural Religion*
David Hume's *The Enquiry for Human Understanding*
Immanuel Kant's *Religion within the Boundaries of Mere Reason*
Immanuel Kant's *Critique of Pure Reason*
Søren Kierkegaard's *The Sickness Unto Death*
Søren Kierkegaard's *Fear and Trembling*
C. S. Lewis's *The Abolition of Man*
Alasdair MacIntyre's *After Virtue*
Marcus Aurelius's *Meditations*
Friedrich Nietzsche's *On the Genealogy of Morality*
Friedrich Nietzsche's *Beyond Good and Evil*
Plato's *Republic*
Plato's *Symposium*
Jean-Jacques Rousseau's *The Social Contract*
Gilbert Ryle's *The Concept of Mind*
Baruch Spinoza's *Ethics*
Sun Tzu's *The Art of War*
Ludwig Wittgenstein's *Philosophical Investigations*

POLITICS

Benedict Anderson's *Imagined Communities*
Aristotle's *Politics*
Bernard Bailyn's *The Ideological Origins of the American Revolution*
Edmund Burke's *Reflections on the Revolution in France*
John C. Calhoun's *A Disquisition on Government*
Ha-Joon Chang's *Kicking Away the Ladder*
Hamid Dabashi's *Iran: A People Interrupted*
Hamid Dabashi's *Theology of Discontent: The Ideological Foundation of the Islamic Revolution in Iran*
Robert Dahl's *Democracy and its Critics*
Robert Dahl's *Who Governs?*
David Brion Davis's *The Problem of Slavery in the Age of Revolution*

The Macat Library By Discipline

Alexis De Tocqueville's *Democracy in America*
James Ferguson's *The Anti-Politics Machine*
Frank Dikötter's *Mao's Great Famine*
Sheila Fitzpatrick's *Everyday Stalinism*
Eric Foner's *Reconstruction: America's Unfinished Revolution, 1863-1877*
Milton Friedman's *Capitalism and Freedom*
Francis Fukuyama's *The End of History and the Last Man*
John Lewis Gaddis's *We Now Know: Rethinking Cold War History*
Ernest Gellner's *Nations and Nationalism*
David Graeber's *Debt: the First 5000 Years*
Antonio Gramsci's *The Prison Notebooks*
Alexander Hamilton, John Jay & James Madison's *The Federalist Papers*
Friedrich Hayek's *The Road to Serfdom*
Christopher Hill's *The World Turned Upside Down*
Thomas Hobbes's *Leviathan*
John A. Hobson's *Imperialism: A Study*
Samuel P. Huntington's *The Clash of Civilizations and the Remaking of World Order*
Tony Judt's *Postwar: A History of Europe Since 1945*
David C. Kang's *China Rising: Peace, Power and Order in East Asia*
Paul Kennedy's *The Rise and Fall of Great Powers*
Robert Keohane's *After Hegemony*
Martin Luther King Jr.'s *Why We Can't Wait*
Henry Kissinger's *World Order: Reflections on the Character of Nations and the Course of History*
John Locke's *Two Treatises of Government*
Niccolò Machiavelli's *The Prince*
Thomas Robert Malthus's *An Essay on the Principle of Population*
Mahmood Mamdani's *Citizen and Subject: Contemporary Africa And The Legacy Of Late Colonialism*
Karl Marx's *Capital*
John Stuart Mill's *On Liberty*
John Stuart Mill's *Utilitarianism*
Hans Morgenthau's *Politics Among Nations*
Thomas Paine's *Common Sense*
Thomas Paine's *Rights of Man*
Thomas Piketty's *Capital in the Twenty-First Century*
Robert D. Putman's *Bowling Alone*
John Rawls's *Theory of Justice*
Jean-Jacques Rousseau's *The Social Contract*
Theda Skocpol's *States and Social Revolutions*
Adam Smith's *The Wealth of Nations*
Sun Tzu's *The Art of War*
Henry David Thoreau's *Civil Disobedience*
Thucydides's *The History of the Peloponnesian War*
Kenneth Waltz's *Theory of International Politics*
Max Weber's *Politics as a Vocation*
Odd Arne Westad's *The Global Cold War: Third World Interventions And The Making Of Our Times*

POSTCOLONIAL STUDIES

Roland Barthes's *Mythologies*
Frantz Fanon's *Black Skin, White Masks*
Homi K. Bhabha's *The Location of Culture*
Gustavo Gutiérrez's *A Theology of Liberation*
Edward Said's *Orientalism*
Gayatri Chakravorty Spivak's *Can the Subaltern Speak?*

PSYCHOLOGY
Gordon Allport's *The Nature of Prejudice*
Alan Baddeley & Graham Hitch's *Aggression: A Social Learning Analysis*
Albert Bandura's *Aggression: A Social Learning Analysis*
Leon Festinger's *A Theory of Cognitive Dissonance*
Sigmund Freud's *The Interpretation of Dreams*
Betty Friedan's *The Feminine Mystique*
Michael R. Gottfredson & Travis Hirschi's *A General Theory of Crime*
Eric Hoffer's *The True Believer: Thoughts on the Nature of Mass Movements*
William James's *Principles of Psychology*
Elizabeth Loftus's *Eyewitness Testimony*
A. H. Maslow's *A Theory of Human Motivation*
Stanley Milgram's *Obedience to Authority*
Steven Pinker's *The Better Angels of Our Nature*
Oliver Sacks's *The Man Who Mistook His Wife For a Hat*
Richard Thaler & Cass Sunstein's *Nudge: Improving Decisions About Health, Wealth and Happiness*
Amos Tversky's *Judgment under Uncertainty: Heuristics and Biases*
Philip Zimbardo's *The Lucifer Effect*

SCIENCE
Rachel Carson's *Silent Spring*
William Cronon's *Nature's Metropolis: Chicago And The Great West*
Alfred W. Crosby's *The Columbian Exchange*
Charles Darwin's *On the Origin of Species*
Richard Dawkin's *The Selfish Gene*
Thomas Kuhn's *The Structure of Scientific Revolutions*
Geoffrey Parker's *Global Crisis: War, Climate Change and Catastrophe in the Seventeenth Century*
Mathis Wackernagel & William Rees's *Our Ecological Footprint*

SOCIOLOGY
Michelle Alexander's *The New Jim Crow: Mass Incarceration in the Age of Colorblindness*
Gordon Allport's *The Nature of Prejudice*
Albert Bandura's *Aggression: A Social Learning Analysis*
Hanna Batatu's *The Old Social Classes And The Revolutionary Movements Of Iraq*
Ha-Joon Chang's *Kicking Away the Ladder*
W. E. B. Du Bois's *The Souls of Black Folk*
Émile Durkheim's *On Suicide*
Frantz Fanon's *Black Skin, White Masks*
Frantz Fanon's *The Wretched of the Earth*
Eric Foner's *Reconstruction: America's Unfinished Revolution, 1863-1877*
Eugene Genovese's *Roll, Jordan, Roll: The World the Slaves Made*
Jack Goldstone's *Revolution and Rebellion in the Early Modern World*
Antonio Gramsci's *The Prison Notebooks*
Richard Herrnstein & Charles A Murray's *The Bell Curve: Intelligence and Class Structure in American Life*
Eric Hoffer's *The True Believer: Thoughts on the Nature of Mass Movements*
Jane Jacobs's *The Death and Life of Great American Cities*
Robert Lucas's *Why Doesn't Capital Flow from Rich to Poor Countries?*
Jay Macleod's *Ain't No Makin' It: Aspirations and Attainment in a Low Income Neighborhood*
Elaine May's *Homeward Bound: American Families in the Cold War Era*
Douglas McGregor's *The Human Side of Enterprise*
C. Wright Mills's *The Sociological Imagination*

Thomas Piketty's *Capital in the Twenty-First Century*
Robert D. Putman's *Bowling Alone*
David Riesman's *The Lonely Crowd: A Study of the Changing American Character*
Edward Said's *Orientalism*
Joan Wallach Scott's *Gender and the Politics of History*
Theda Skocpol's *States and Social Revolutions*
Max Weber's *The Protestant Ethic and the Spirit of Capitalism*

THEOLOGY

Augustine's *Confessions*
Benedict's *Rule of St Benedict*
Gustavo Gutiérrez's *A Theology of Liberation*
Carole Hillenbrand's *The Crusades: Islamic Perspectives*
David Hume's *Dialogues Concerning Natural Religion*
Immanuel Kant's *Religion within the Boundaries of Mere Reason*
Ernst Kantorowicz's *The King's Two Bodies: A Study in Medieval Political Theology*
Søren Kierkegaard's *The Sickness Unto Death*
C. S. Lewis's *The Abolition of Man*
Saba Mahmood's *The Politics of Piety: The Islamic Revival and the Feminist Subject*
Baruch Spinoza's *Ethics*
Keith Thomas's *Religion and the Decline of Magic*

COMING SOON

Chris Argyris's *The Individual and the Organisation*
Seyla Benhabib's *The Rights of Others*
Walter Benjamin's *The Work Of Art in the Age of Mechanical Reproduction*
John Berger's *Ways of Seeing*
Pierre Bourdieu's *Outline of a Theory of Practice*
Mary Douglas's *Purity and Danger*
Roland Dworkin's *Taking Rights Seriously*
James G. March's *Exploration and Exploitation in Organisational Learning*
Ikujiro Nonaka's *A Dynamic Theory of Organizational Knowledge Creation*
Griselda Pollock's *Vision and Difference*
Amartya Sen's *Inequality Re-Examined*
Susan Sontag's *On Photography*
Yasser Tabbaa's *The Transformation of Islamic Art*
Ludwig von Mises's *Theory of Money and Credit*

Macat Disciplines

Access the greatest ideas and thinkers across entire disciplines, including

AFRICANA STUDIES

Chinua Achebe's *An Image of Africa: Racism in Conrad's Heart of Darkness*

W. E. B. Du Bois's *The Souls of Black Folk*

Zora Neale Hurston's *Characteristics of Negro Expression*

Martin Luther King Jr.'s *Why We Can't Wait*

Toni Morrison's *Playing in the Dark: Whiteness in the American Literary Imagination*

Macat analyses are available from all good bookshops and libraries.

Access hundreds of analyses through one, multimedia tool.
Join free for one month **library.macat.com**

Macat Disciplines

Access the greatest ideas and thinkers across entire disciplines, including

FEMINISM, GENDER AND QUEER STUDIES

Simone De Beauvoir's
The Second Sex

Michel Foucault's
History of Sexuality

Betty Friedan's
The Feminine Mystique

Saba Mahmood's
The Politics of Piety: The Islamic Revival and the Feminist Subject

Joan Wallach Scott's
Gender and the Politics of History

Mary Wollstonecraft's
A Vindication of the Rights of Woman

Virginia Woolf's
A Room of One's Own

Judith Butler's
Gender Trouble

Macat Disciplines

Access the greatest ideas and thinkers across entire disciplines, including

INEQUALITY

Ha-Joon Chang's, *Kicking Away the Ladder*

David Graeber's, *Debt: The First 5000 Years*

Robert E. Lucas's, *Why Doesn't Capital Flow from Rich To Poor Countries?*

Thomas Piketty's, *Capital in the Twenty-First Century*

Amartya Sen's, *Inequality Re-Examined*

Mahbub Ul Haq's, *Reflections on Human Development*

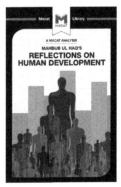

Macat analyses are available from all good bookshops and libraries.

Access hundreds of analyses through one, multimedia tool.
Join free for one month **library.macat.com**

Macat Disciplines

Access the greatest ideas and thinkers across entire disciplines, including

CRIMINOLOGY

Michelle Alexander's
The New Jim Crow: Mass Incarceration in the Age of Colorblindness

Michael R. Gottfredson & Travis Hirschi's
A General Theory of Crime

Elizabeth Loftus's
Eyewitness Testimony

Richard Herrnstein & Charles A. Murray's
The Bell Curve: Intelligence and Class Structure in American Life

Jay Macleod's
Ain't No Makin' It: Aspirations and Attainment in a Low-Income Neighborhood

Philip Zimbardo's
The Lucifer Effect

Macat analyses are available from all good bookshops and libraries.

Access hundreds of analyses through one, multimedia tool.
Join free for one month **library.macat.com**

Macat Disciplines

Access the greatest ideas and thinkers across entire disciplines, including

Postcolonial Studies

Roland Barthes's *Mythologies*
Frantz Fanon's *Black Skin, White Masks*
Homi K. Bhabha's *The Location of Culture*
Gustavo Gutiérrez's *A Theology of Liberation*
Edward Said's *Orientalism*
Gayatri Chakravorty Spivak's *Can the Subaltern Speak?*

Macat analyses are available from all good bookshops and libraries.

Access hundreds of analyses through one, multimedia tool.
Join free for one month **library.macat.com**

Macat Pairs

Analyse historical and modern issues from opposite sides of an argument. Pairs include:

HOW TO RUN AN ECONOMY

John Maynard Keynes's
The General Theory OF Employment, Interest and Money

Classical economics suggests that market economies are self-correcting in times of recession or depression, and tend toward full employment and output. But English economist John Maynard Keynes disagrees.

In his ground-breaking 1936 study *The General Theory*, Keynes argues that traditional economics has misunderstood the causes of unemployment. Employment is not determined by the price of labor; it is directly linked to demand. Keynes believes market economies are by nature unstable, and so require government intervention. Spurred on by the social catastrophe of the Great Depression of the 1930s, he sets out to revolutionize the way the world thinks

Milton Friedman's
The Role of Monetary Policy

Friedman's 1968 paper changed the course of economic theory. In just 17 pages, he demolished existing theory and outlined an effective alternate monetary policy designed to secure 'high employment, stable prices and rapid growth.'

Friedman demonstrated that monetary policy plays a vital role in broader economic stability and argued that economists got their monetary policy wrong in the 1950s and 1960s by misunderstanding the relationship between inflation and unemployment. Previous generations of economists had believed that governments could permanently decrease unemployment by permitting inflation—and vice versa. Friedman's most original contribution was to show that this supposed trade-off is an illusion that only works in the short term.

Macat analyses are available from all good bookshops and libraries.

Access hundreds of analyses through one, multimedia tool. Join free for one month **library.macat.com**

Macat Disciplines

Access the greatest ideas and thinkers across entire disciplines, including

THE FUTURE OF DEMOCRACY

Robert A. Dahl's, *Democracy and Its Critics*
Robert A. Dahl's, *Who Governs?*
Alexis De Toqueville's, *Democracy in America*
Niccolò Machiavelli's, *The Prince*
John Stuart Mill's, *On Liberty*
Robert D. Putnam's, *Bowling Alone*
Jean-Jacques Rousseau's, *The Social Contract*
Henry David Thoreau's, *Civil Disobedience*

Macat Disciplines

Access the greatest ideas and thinkers across entire disciplines, including

TOTALITARIANISM

Sheila Fitzpatrick's, *Everyday Stalinism*
Ian Kershaw's, *The "Hitler Myth"*
Timothy Snyder's, *Bloodlands*

Macat analyses are available from all good bookshops and libraries.

Access hundreds of analyses through one, multimedia tool.
Join free for one month **library.macat.com**

Printed in the United States
by Baker & Taylor Publisher Services